Oneloa Beach

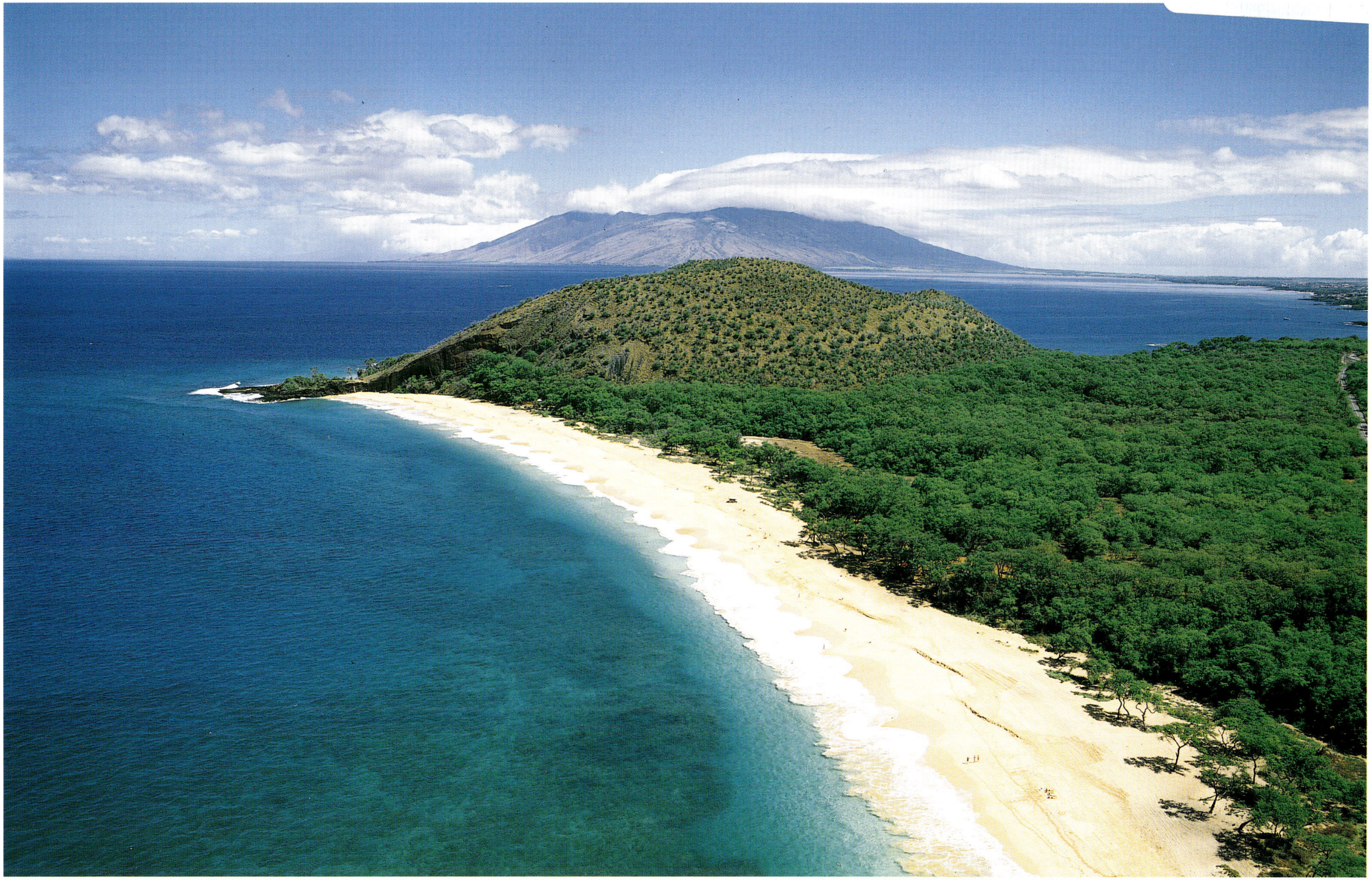

Oneloa Beach well-deserves both its Hawaiian meaning of "long sand" and its English nickname "Big Beach" with its sprawling reach to the cinder cone of Puʻu ʻŌlai. The world-known beaches of the Mākena area offer excellent swimming, snorkeling and sunbathing.

Wailea

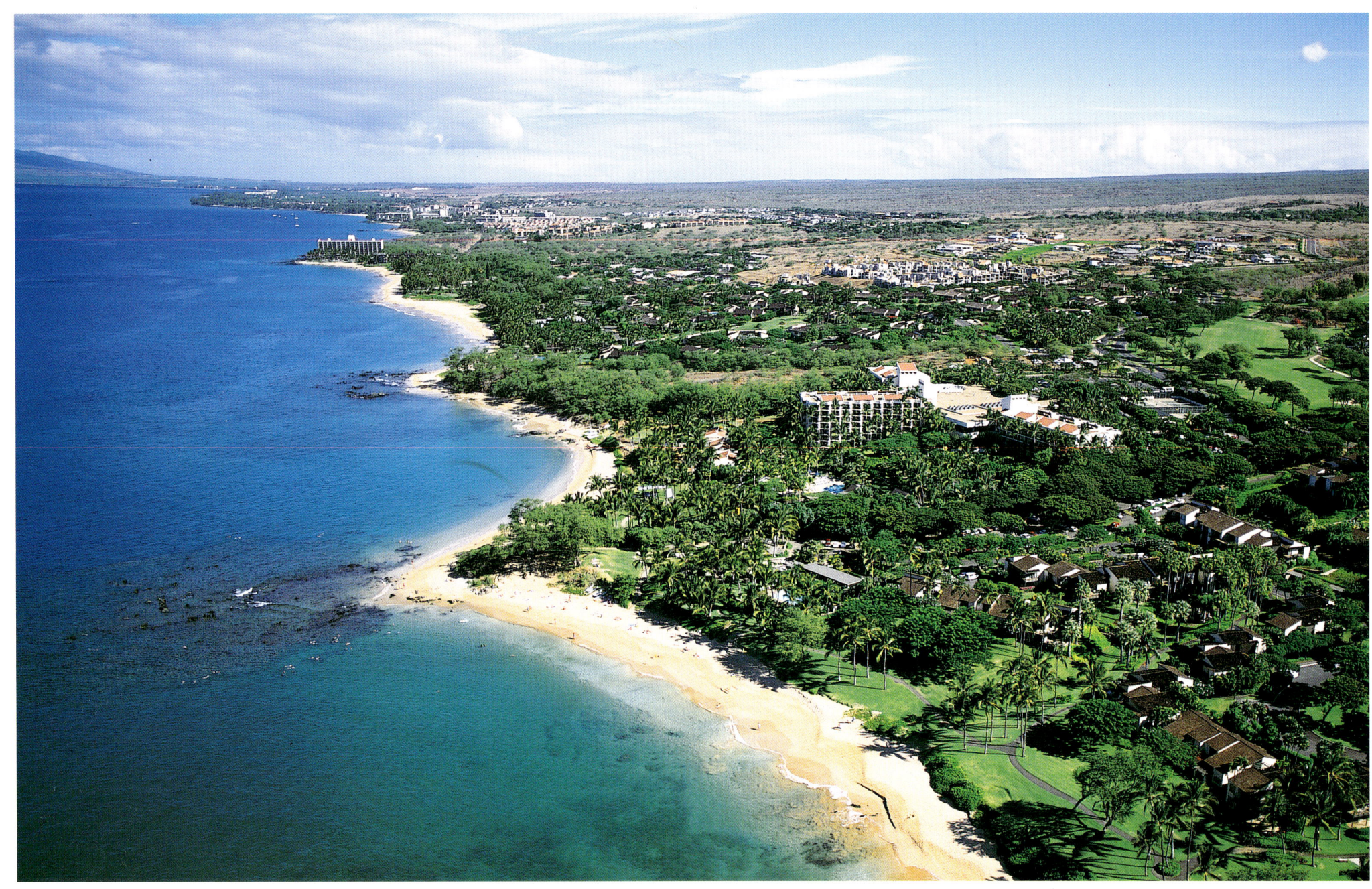

Visitors and kamaʻāina alike relax and play at Wailea with its pristine beaches and luxurious resort surroundings.

Māʻalaea Bay

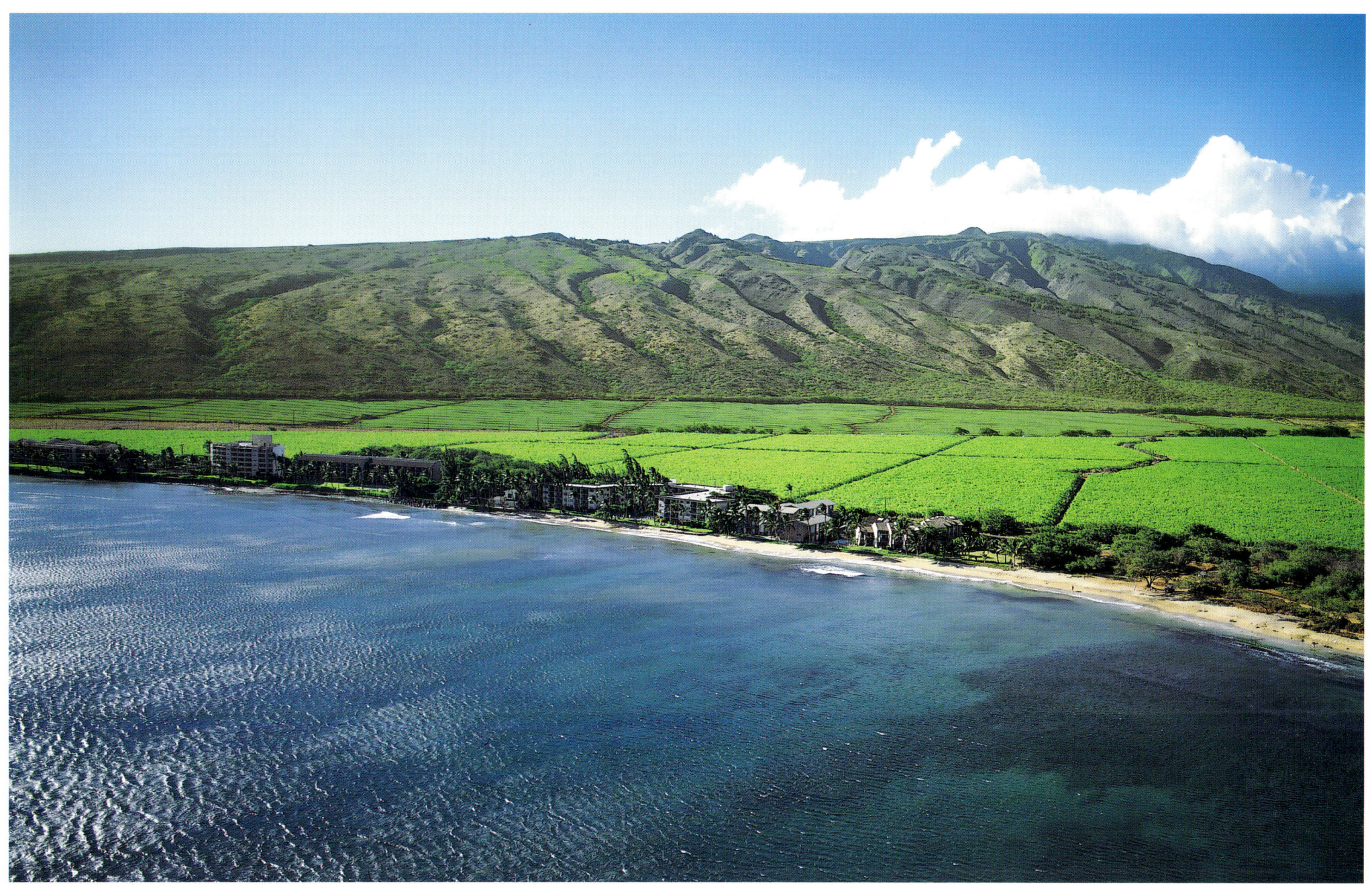

Condominiums catering to sun-loving visitors and residents now line the southern edge of central Maui at the former fishing village of Māʻalaea.

Kīhei

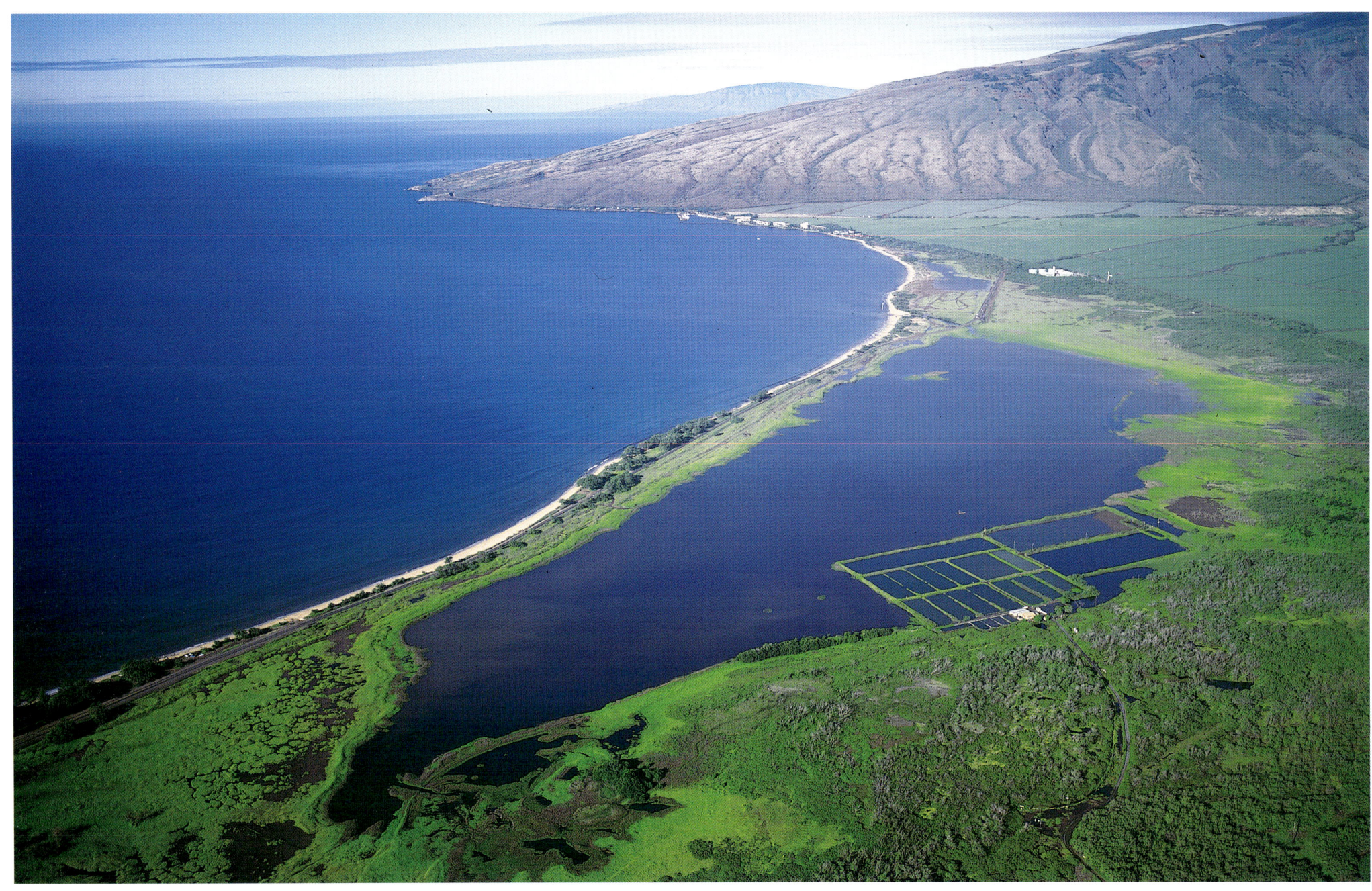

Not far from the bustling beach town of Kīhei, 500-acre Keālia Pond serves as a wildlife refuge for Maui's native birds.

Lahaina

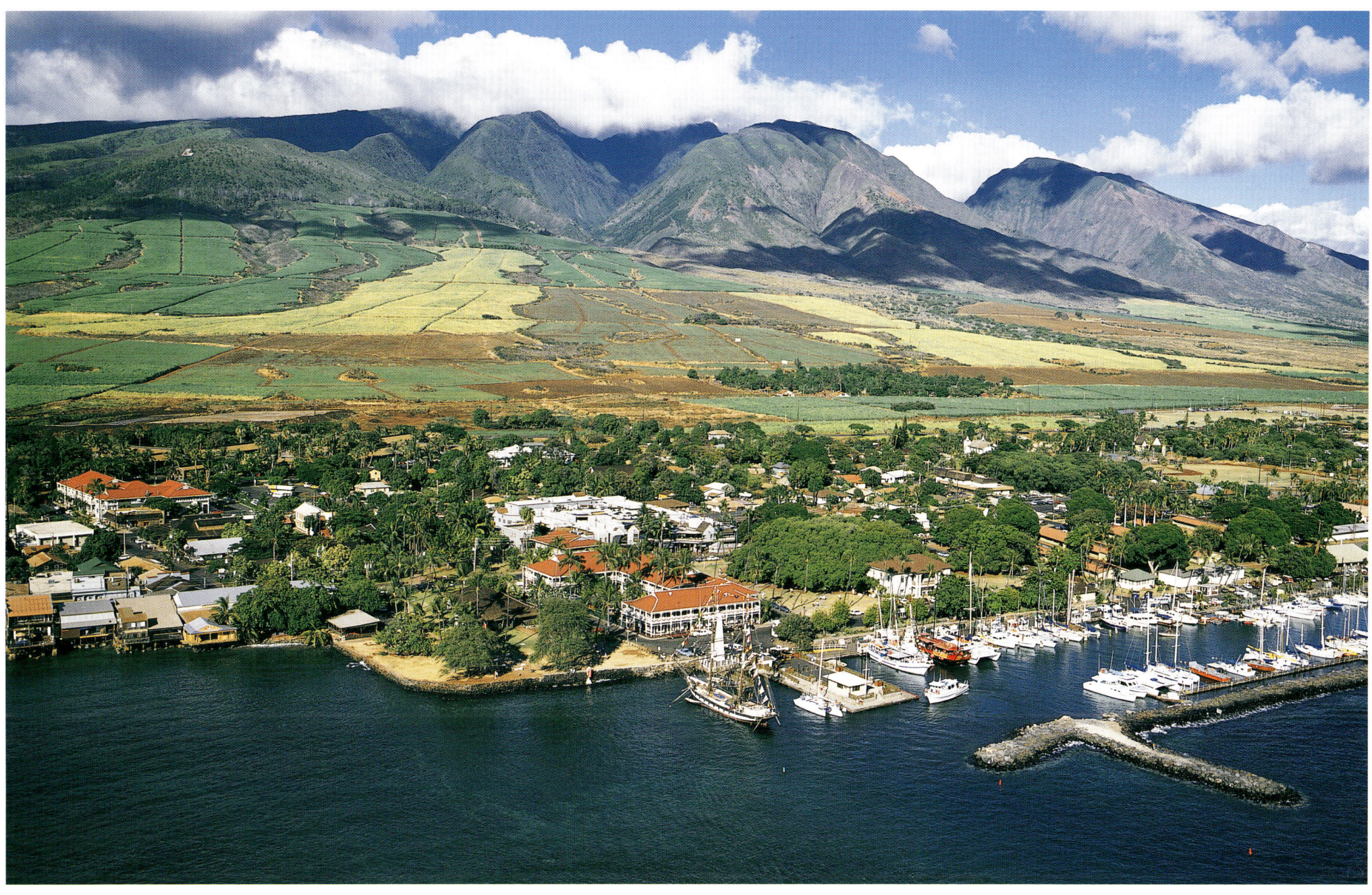

In the 19th century, both bawdy whalers and Hawaiian royalty favored the sunny days and balmy nights at Lahaina. The charms of this historic seaside town continue to lure visitors from around the world.

West Maui Mountains

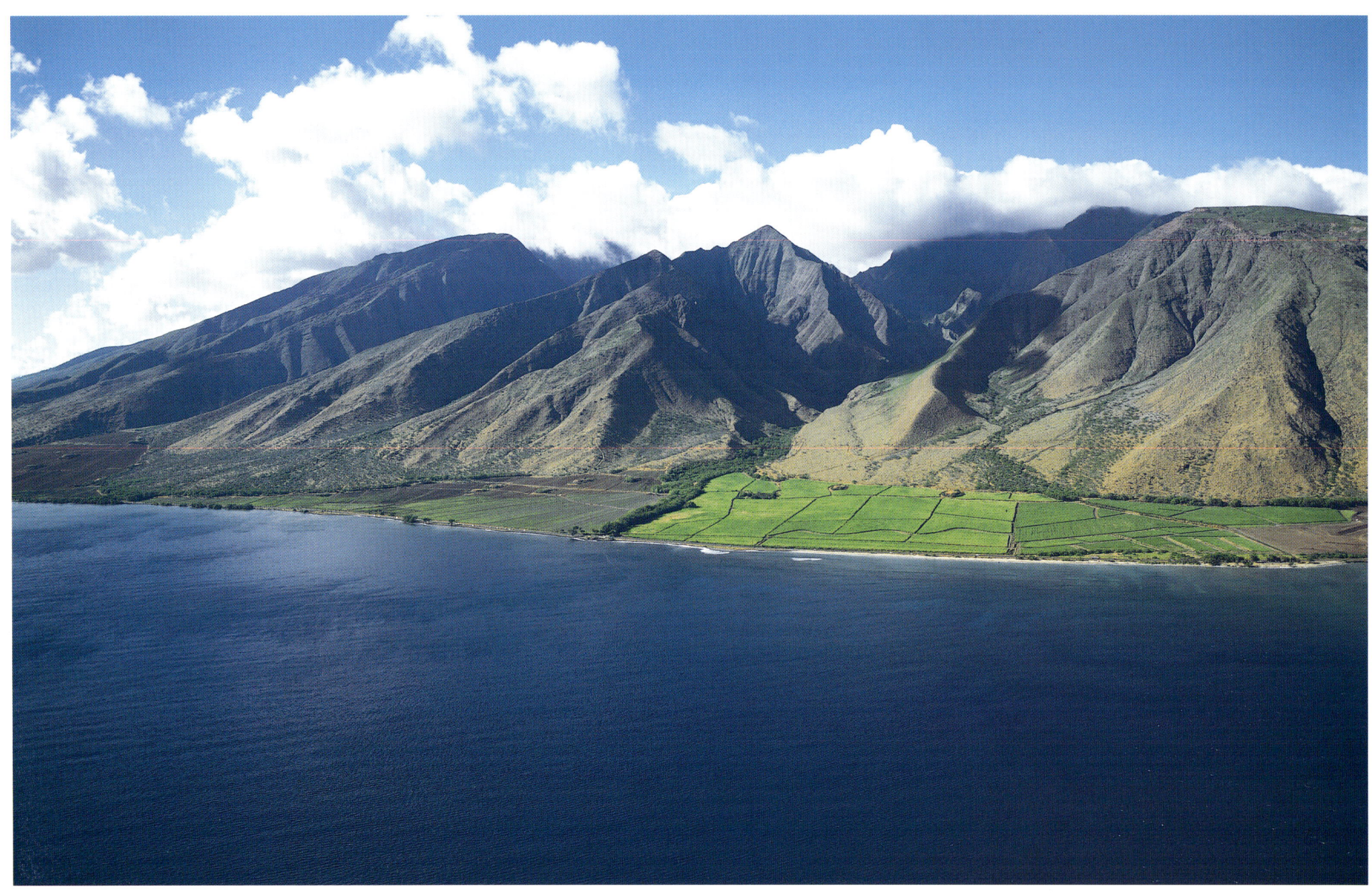

Sunlight accentuates the ridges of the West Maui Mountains, volcanic peaks sliced by water-formed valleys.

ʻĪao Valley

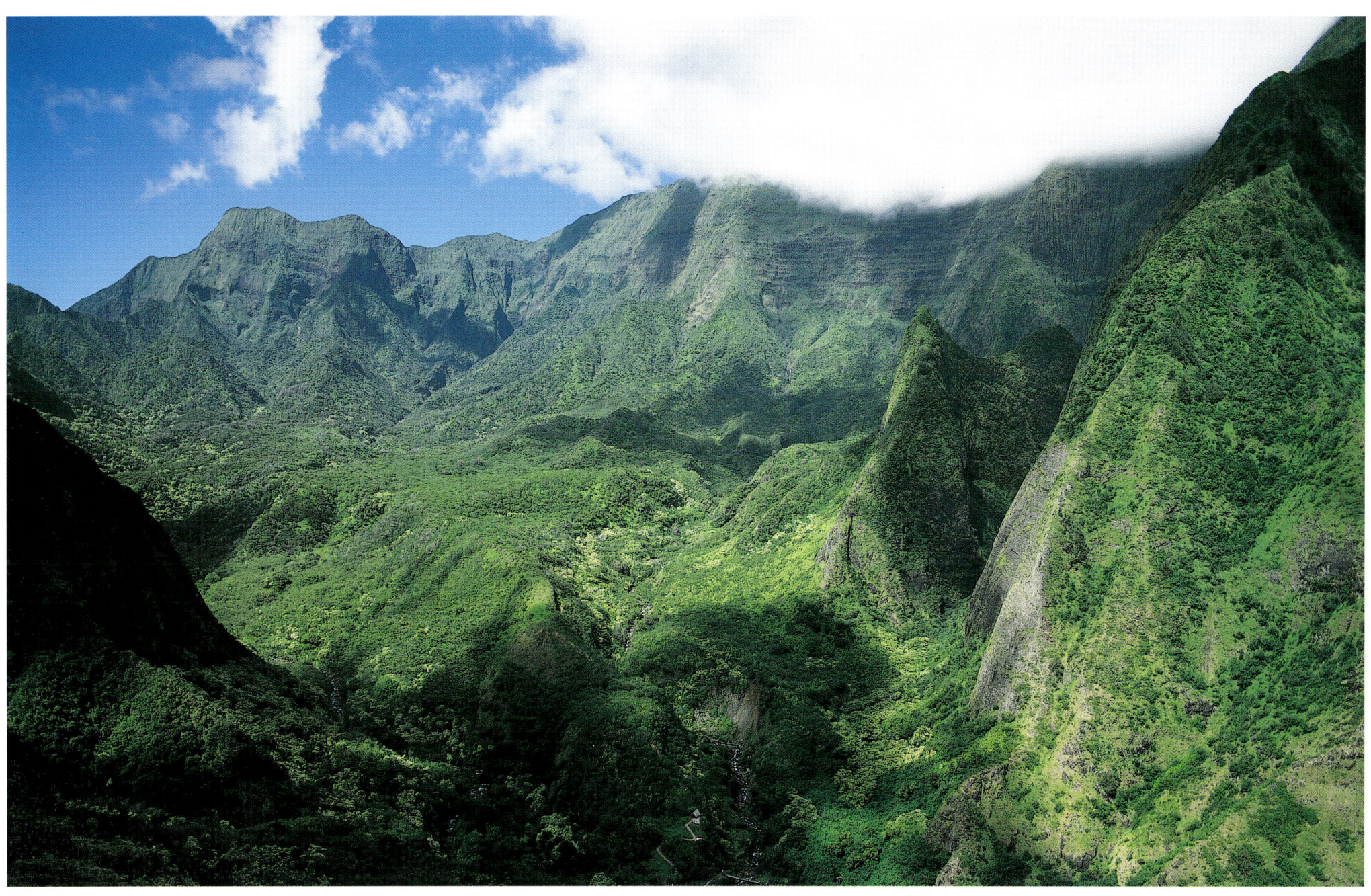

ʻĪao Valley, a sacred burial site for Hawaiian chiefs, cuts deeply into the West Maui Mountains. The home of famous ʻĪao Needle, the valley ends in a vast natural amphitheater surrounded by soaring cliffs.

Kāʻanapali

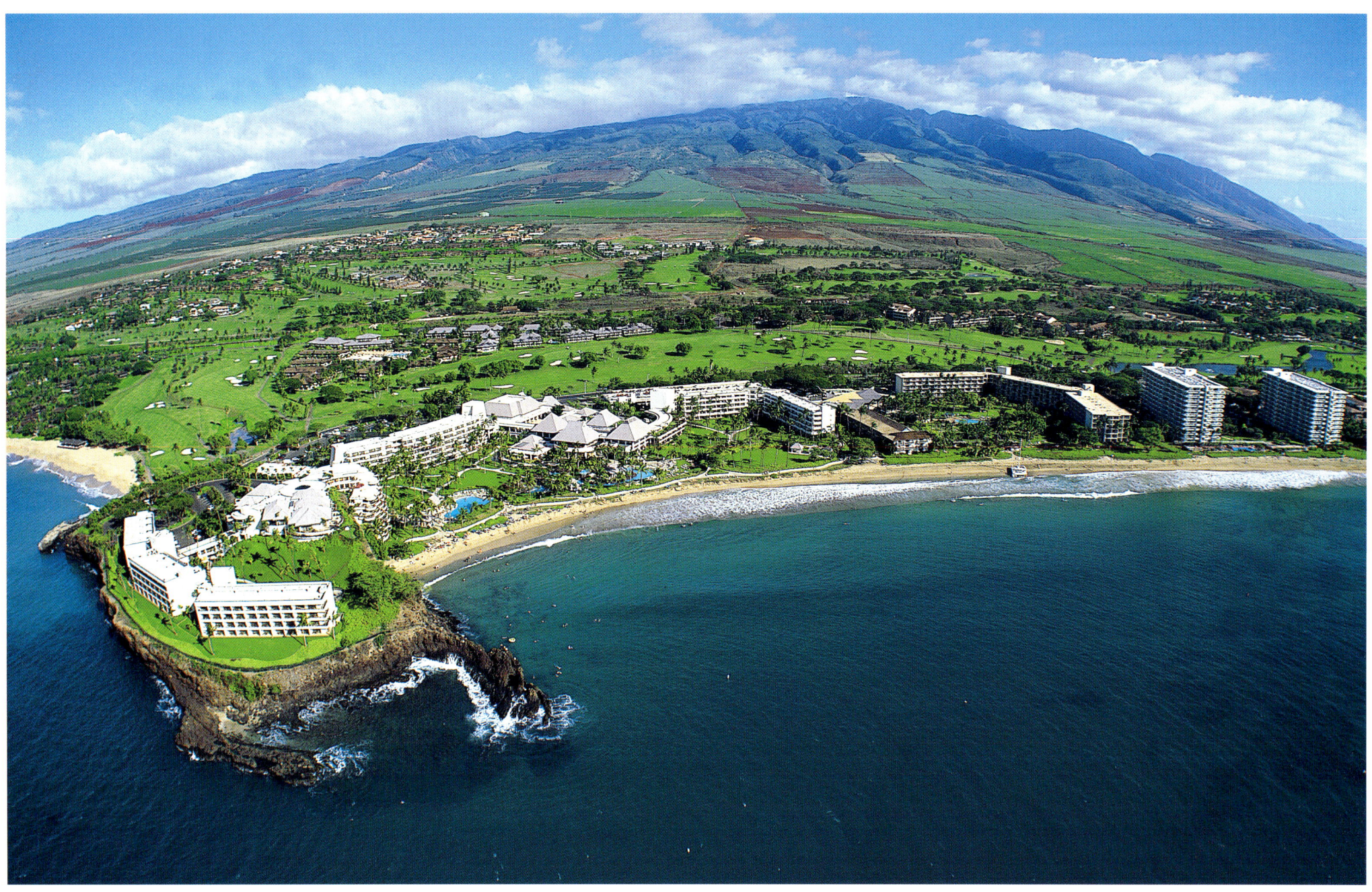

Black Rock, once a "jumping off" place for Hawaiian souls, stands out among three miles of golden Kāʻanapali beaches.

Kapalua

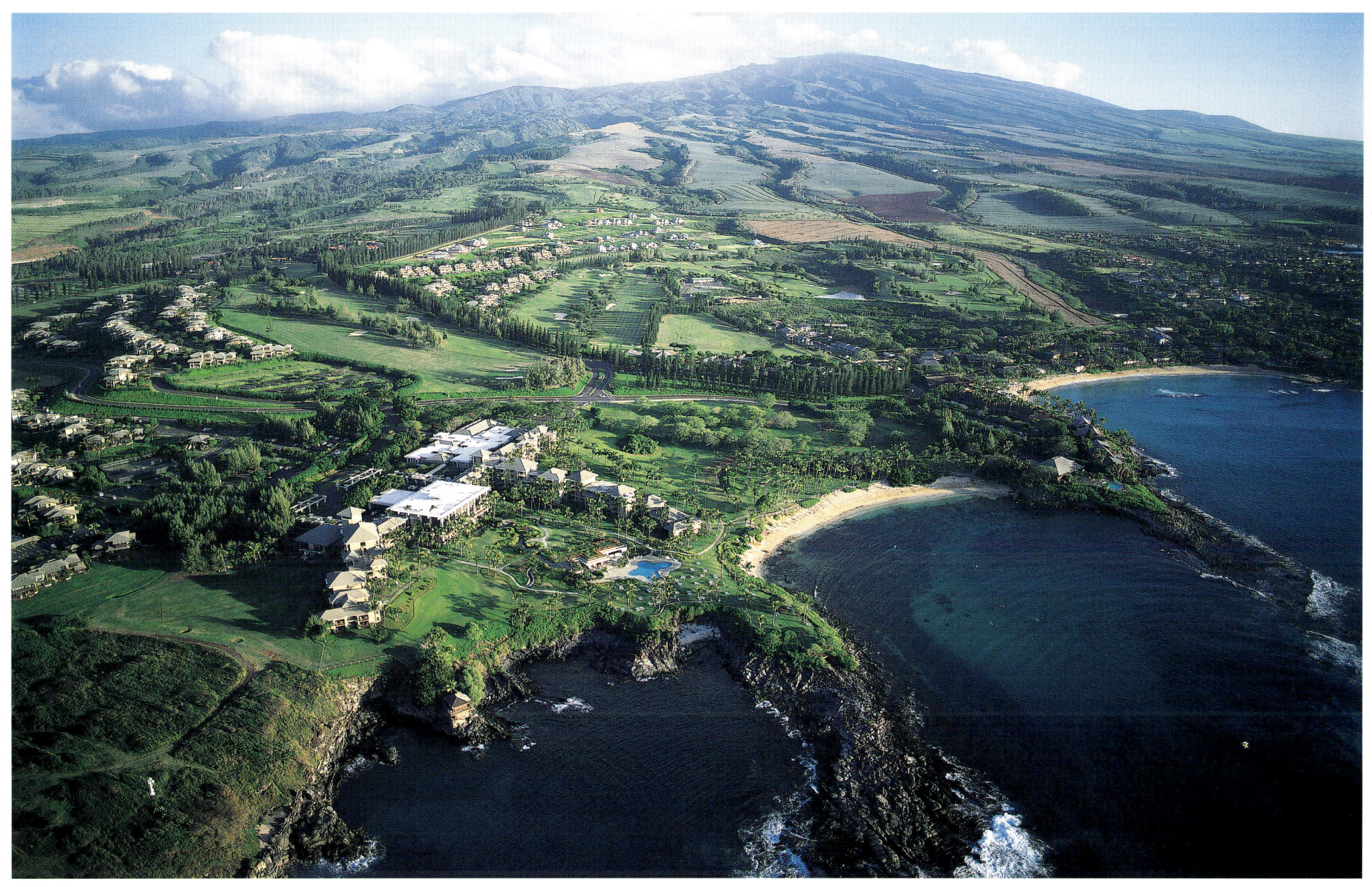

Once a pineapple plantation, Kapalua has been transformed into a luxury resort and residential community, complete with fine dining, golf, and tennis.

Honolua Bay

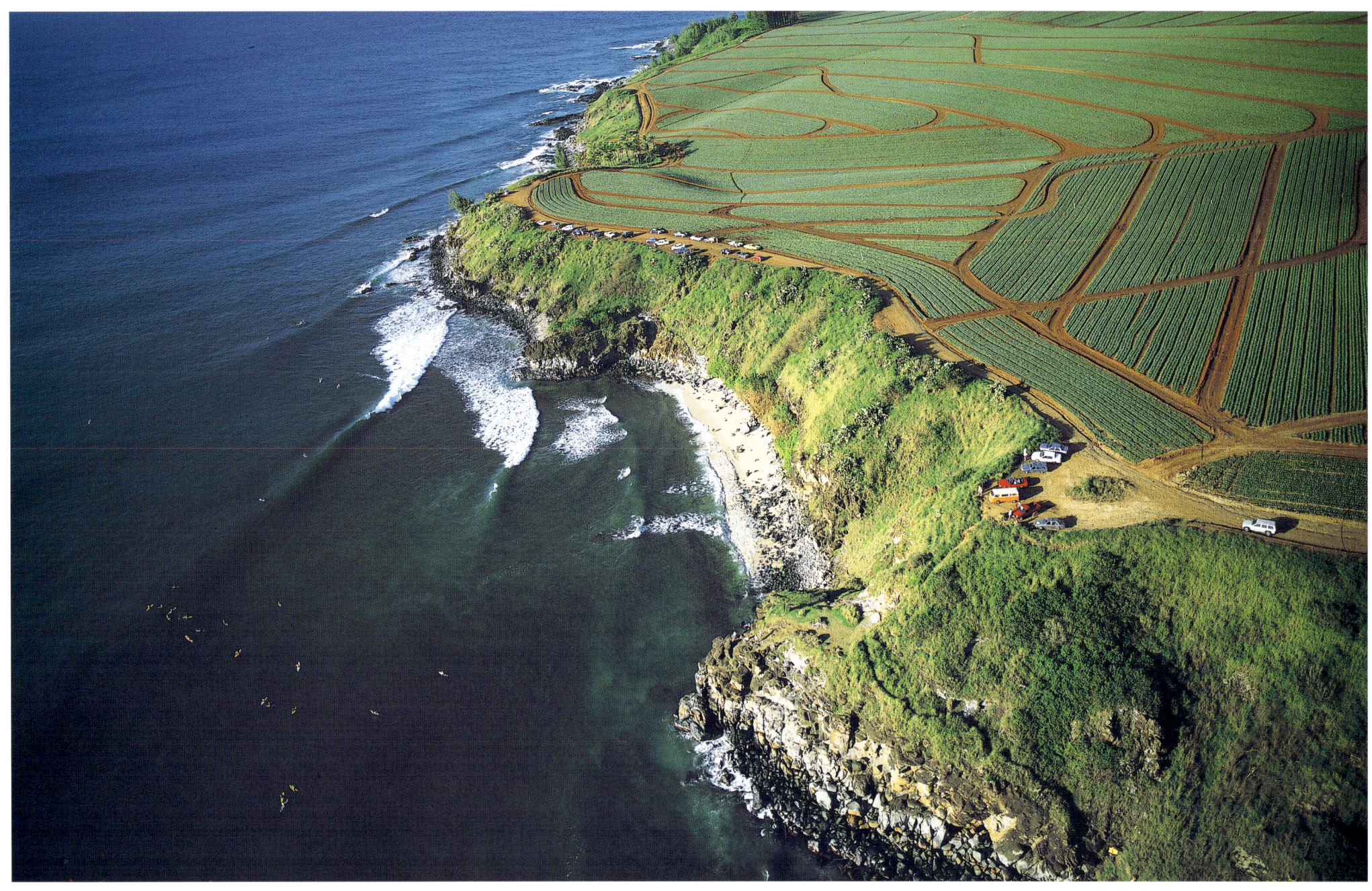

Honolua Bay, located near the Kapalua resort, boasts some of the finest winter surfing in the world.

Kahakuloa Bay

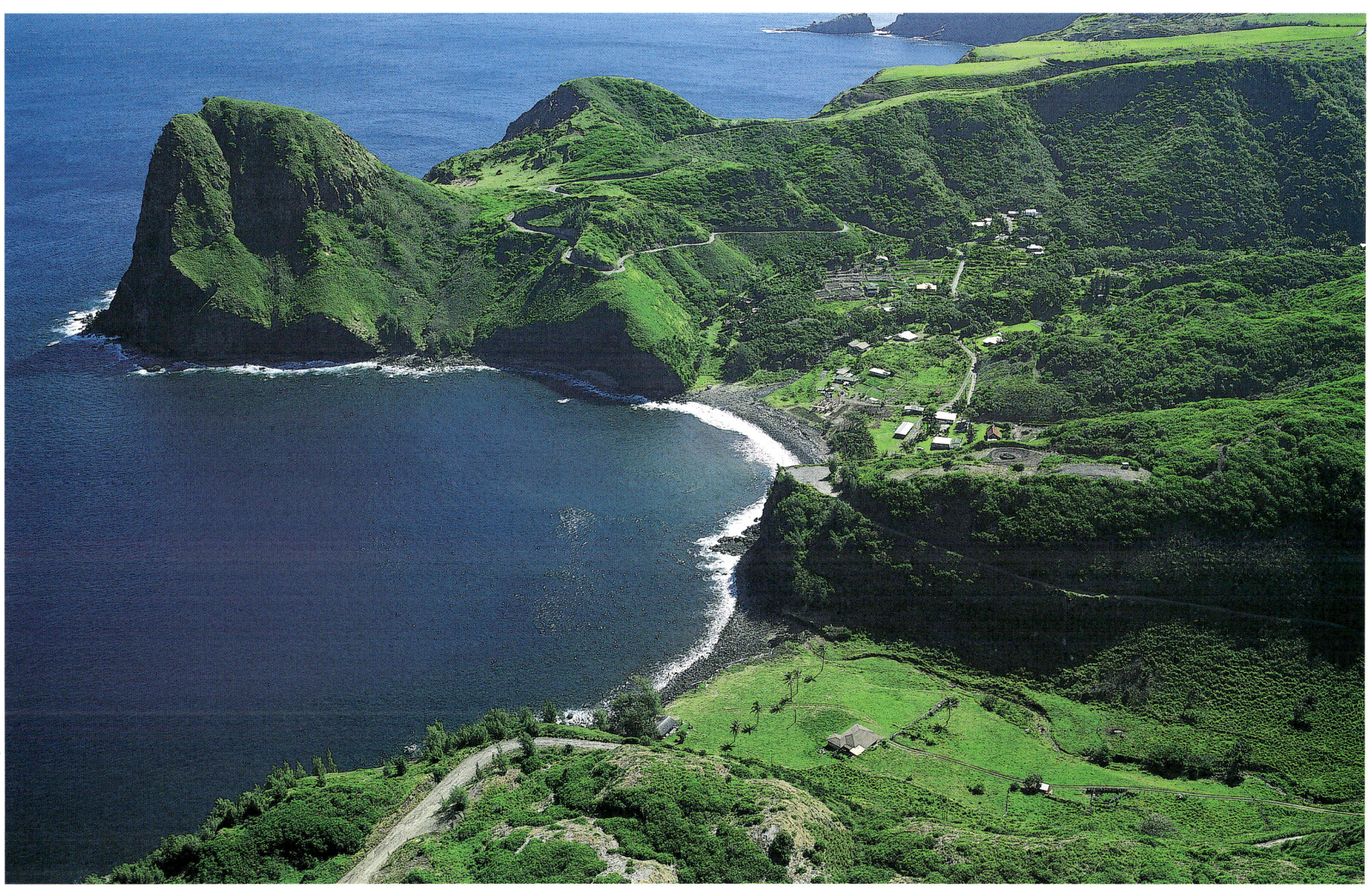

Rugged Kahakuloa Head dominates the remote village of Kahakuloa. Here taro farmers utilize traditional methods of cultivation.

Kahakuloa Road

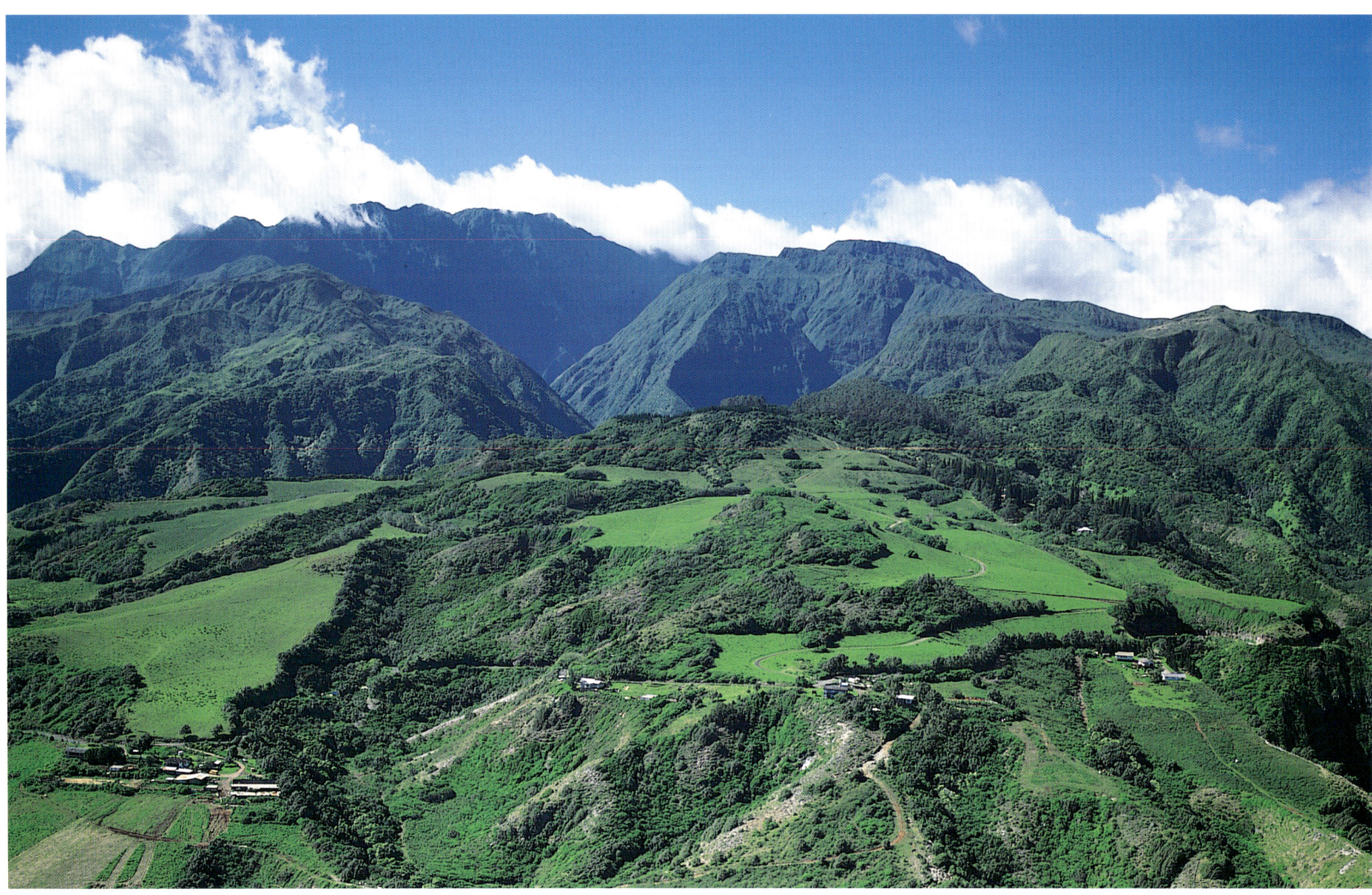

Scenic but treacherous, the road to Kahakuloa snakes through verdant pastures alongside plunging cliffs.

Wailuku

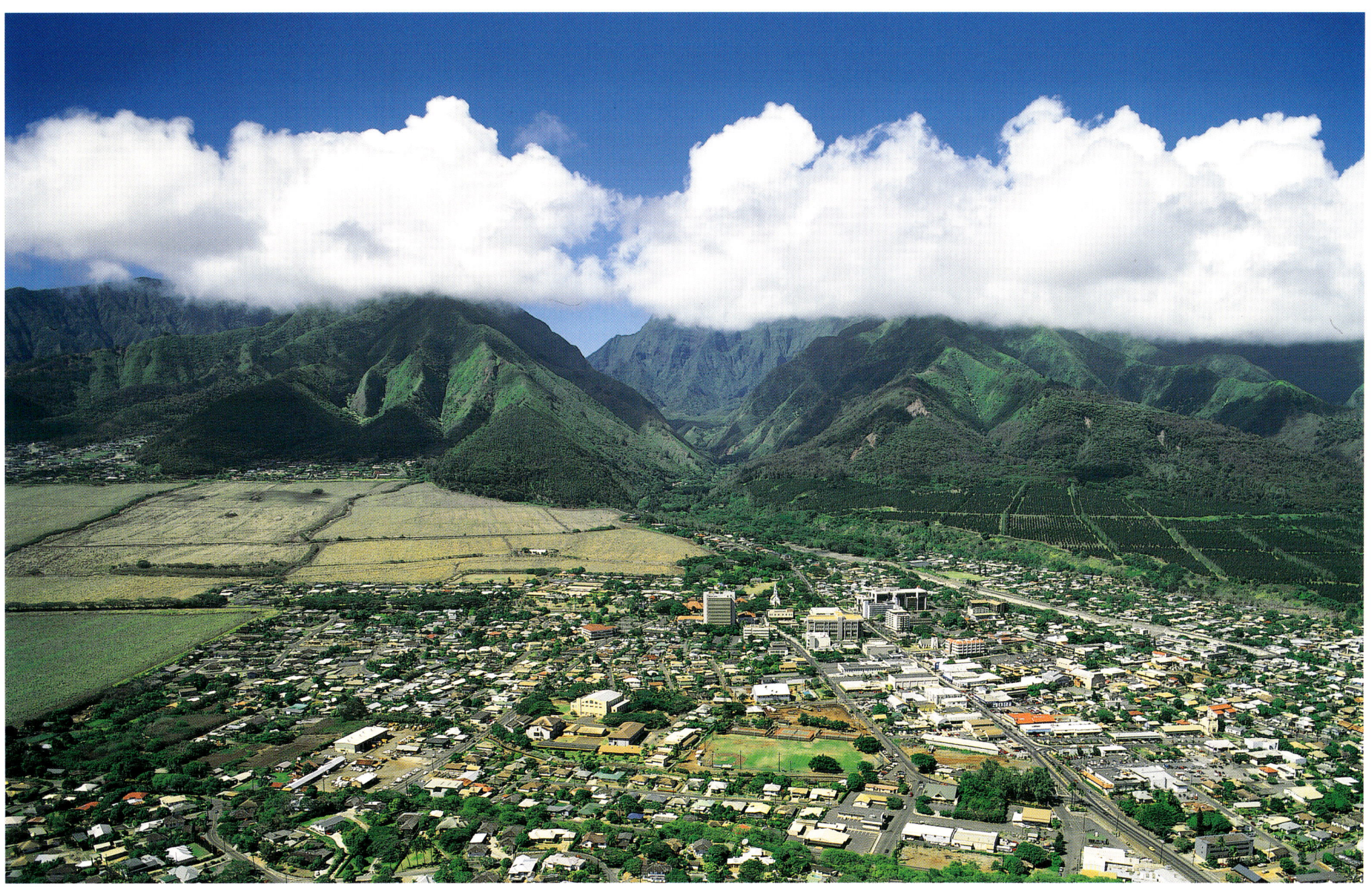

Wailuku, along with sister city Kahului, forms Central Maui's residential and commercial hub. A former plantation town, Wailuku provides a glimpse into old time Maui.

Ho‘okipa Beach Park

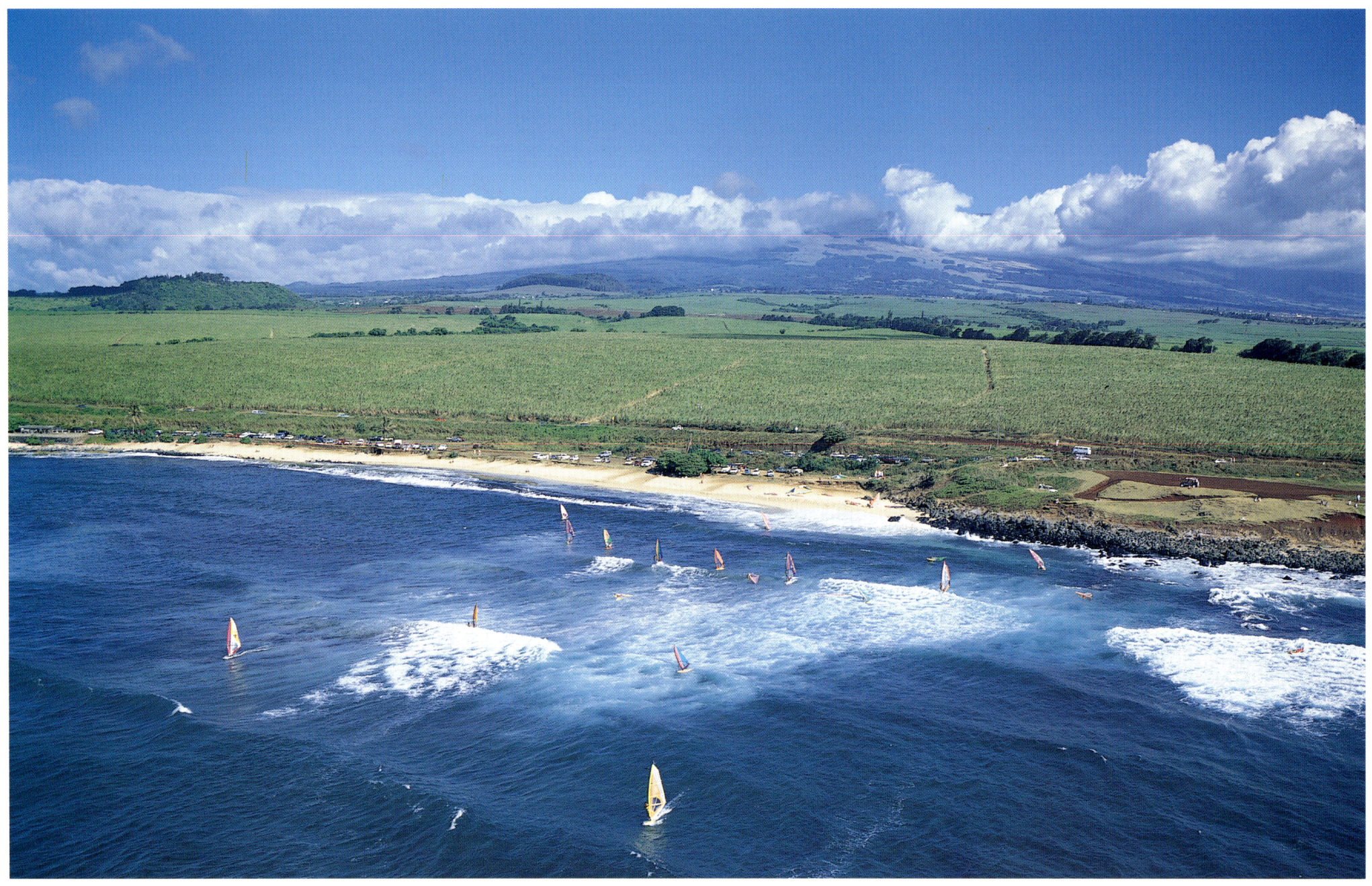

Brilliantly-colored sails skimming over the water create an ever-changing ocean canvas at Ho‘okipa Beach Park.

Ke'anae Valley

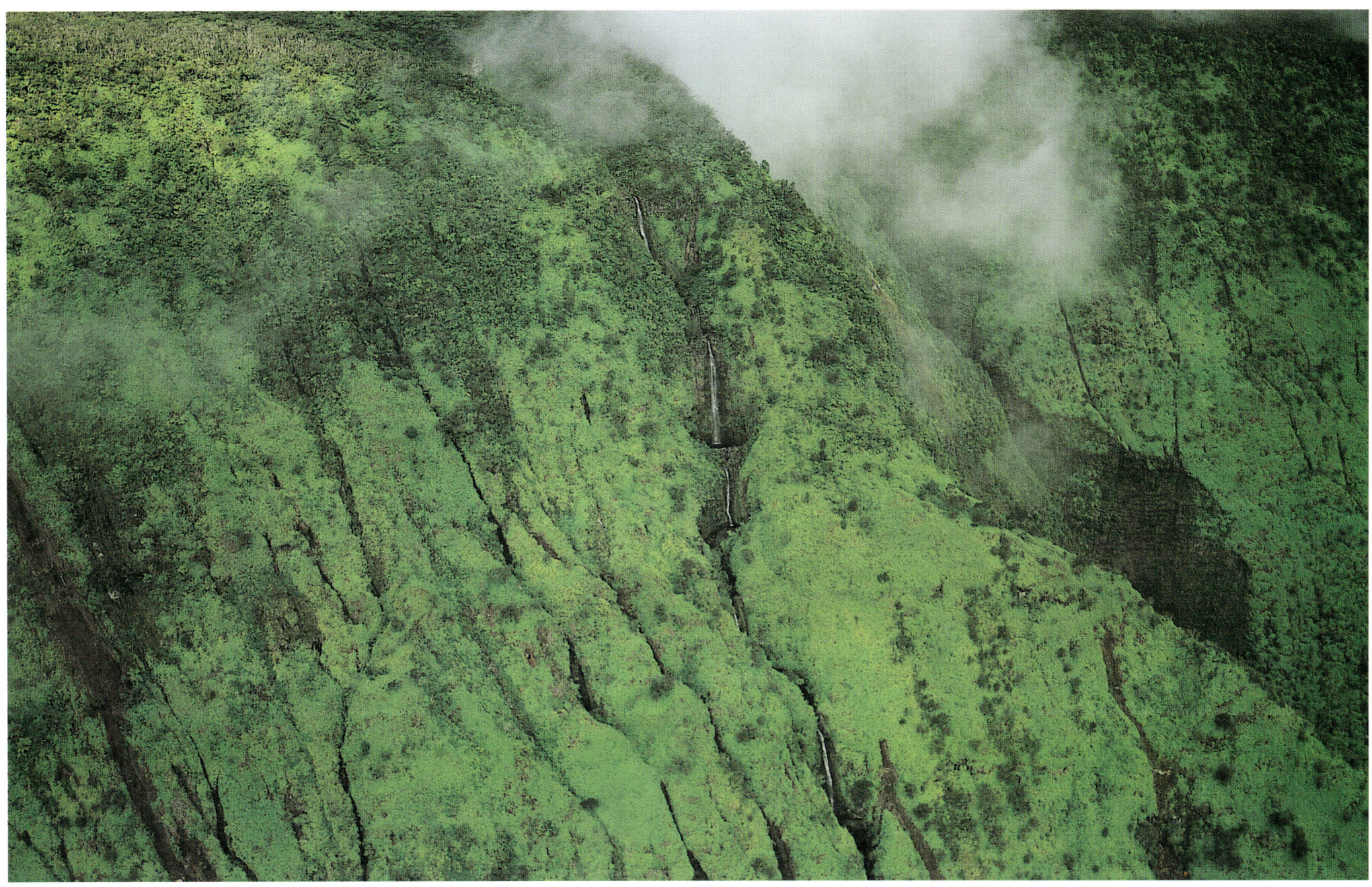

Water flows abundantly from the north flank of Haleakalā through Ke'anae Valley to the Hāna coast.

Ke'anae Peninsula

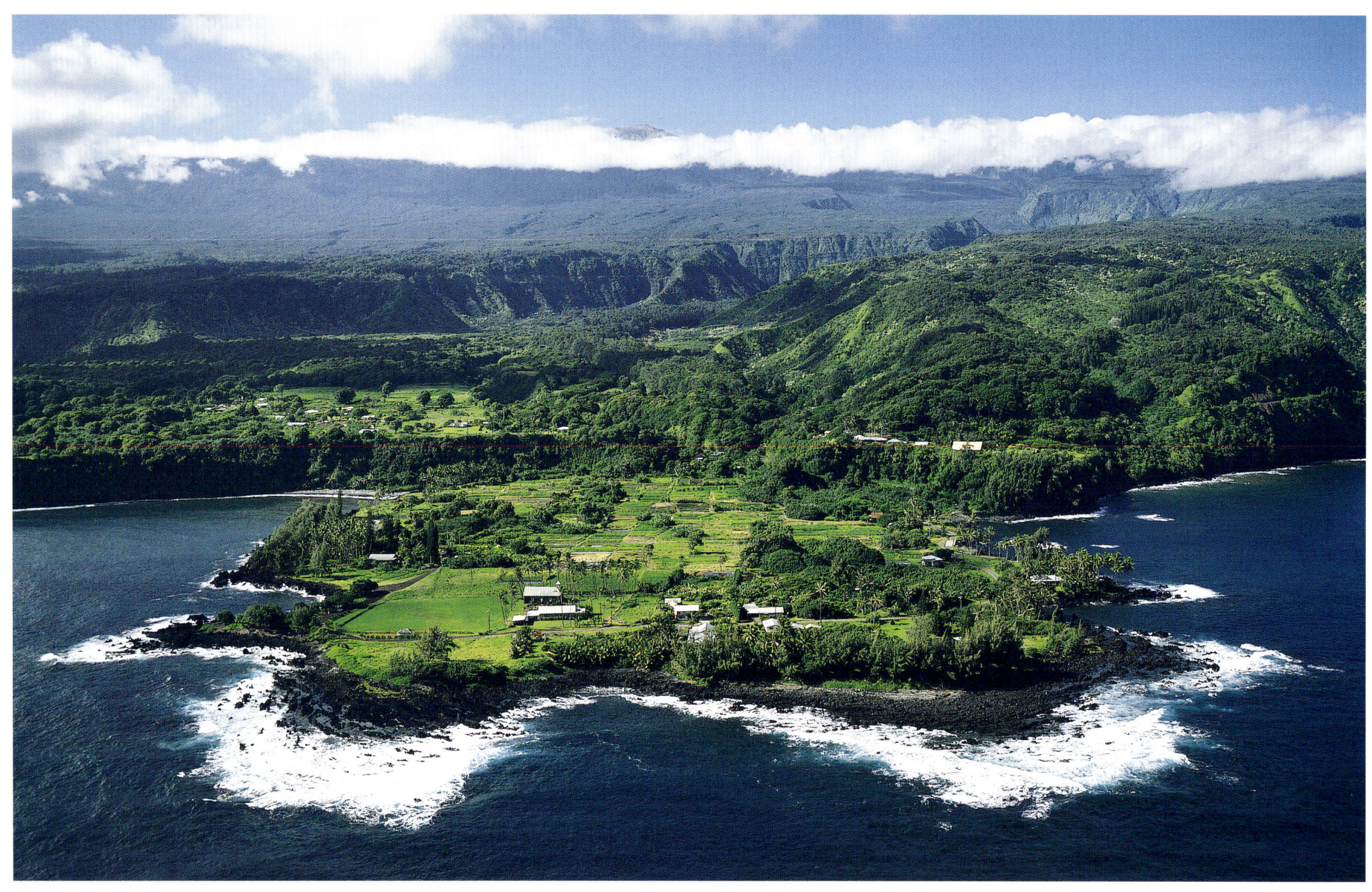

The idyllic village of Ke'anae brings Maui's past to life with its historic church, taro patches, and Hawaiian-style homes.

Haleakalā

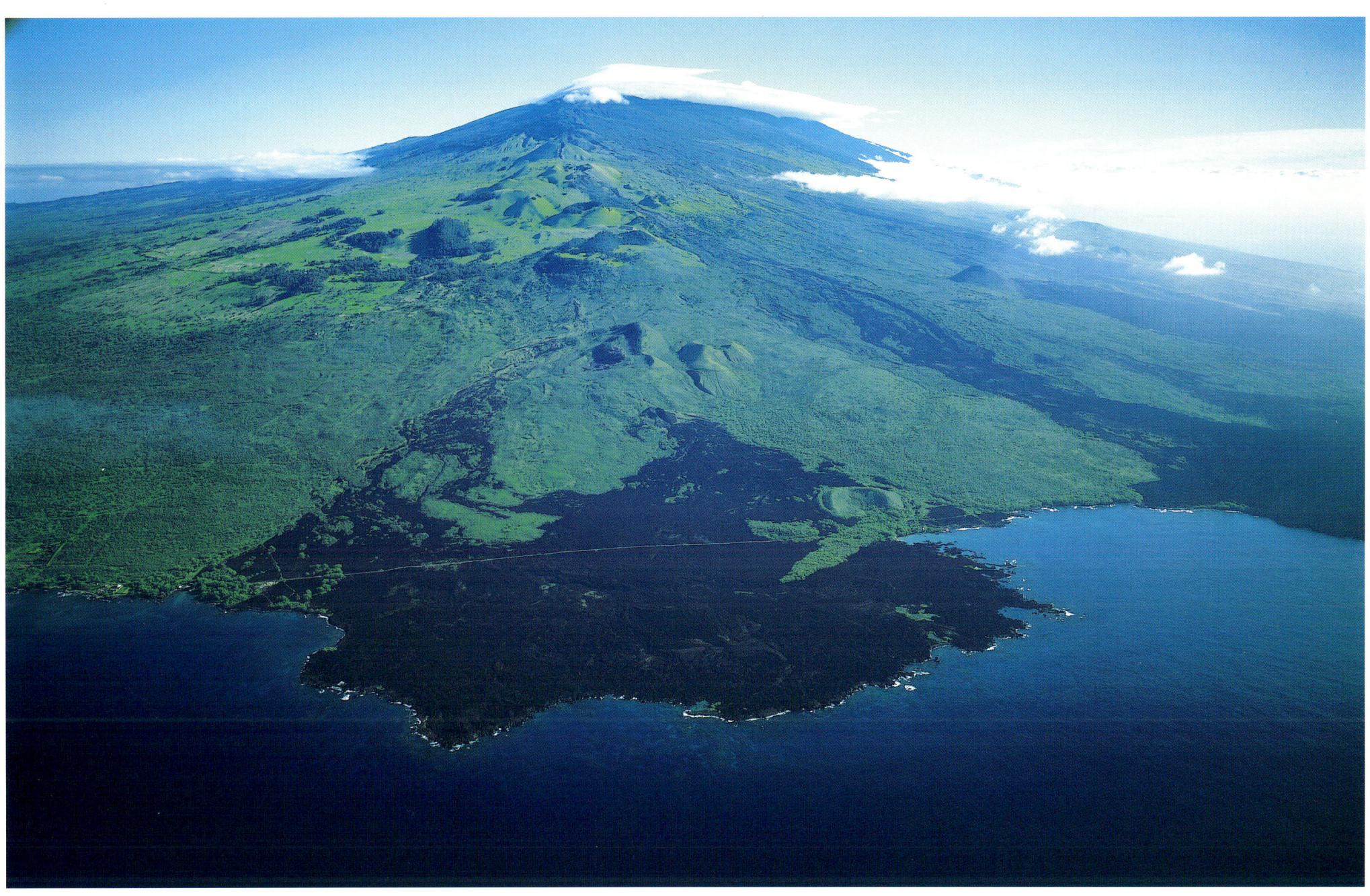

The green sheen of Haleakalā's southern slope ends at the black terrain of Cape Kīna'u, young lava deposited by Maui's last eruption in 1790.

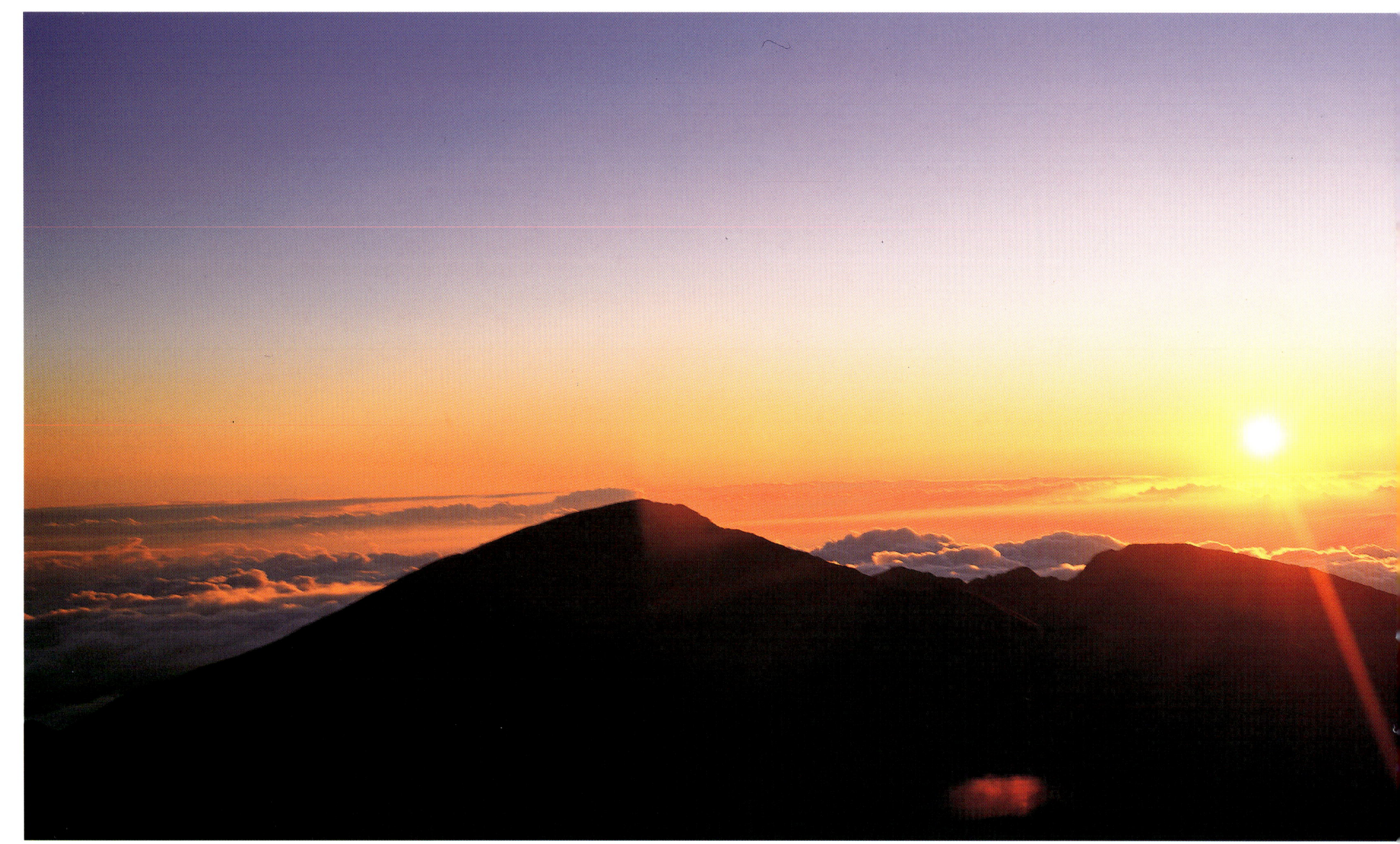

Haleakalā

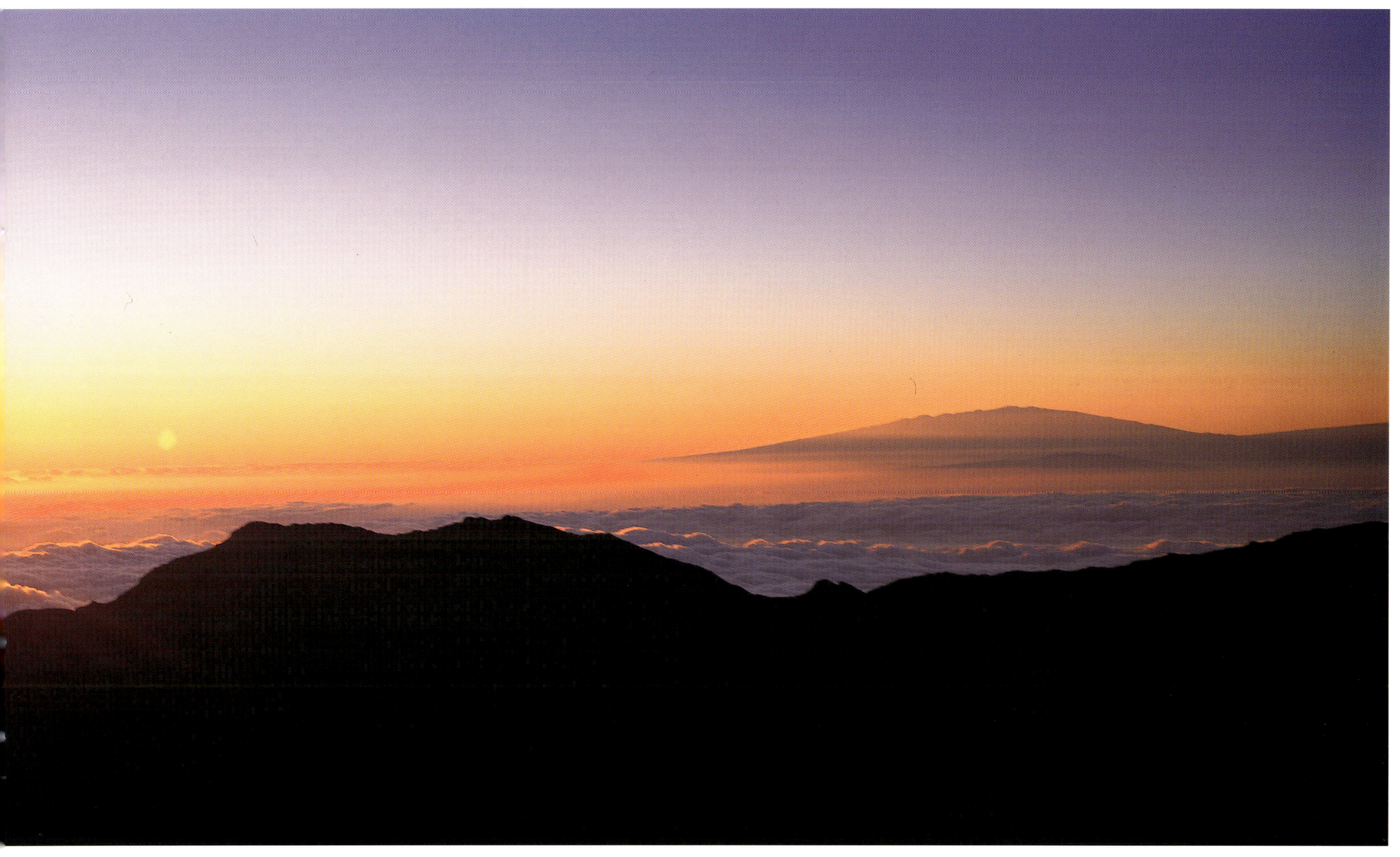

The sun rises majestically over Haleakalā, with sister volcano Mauna Kea on the Big Island of Hawai'i in the distance. Thousands rise long before dawn each year to experience this solar spectacle.

Road to Haleakalā

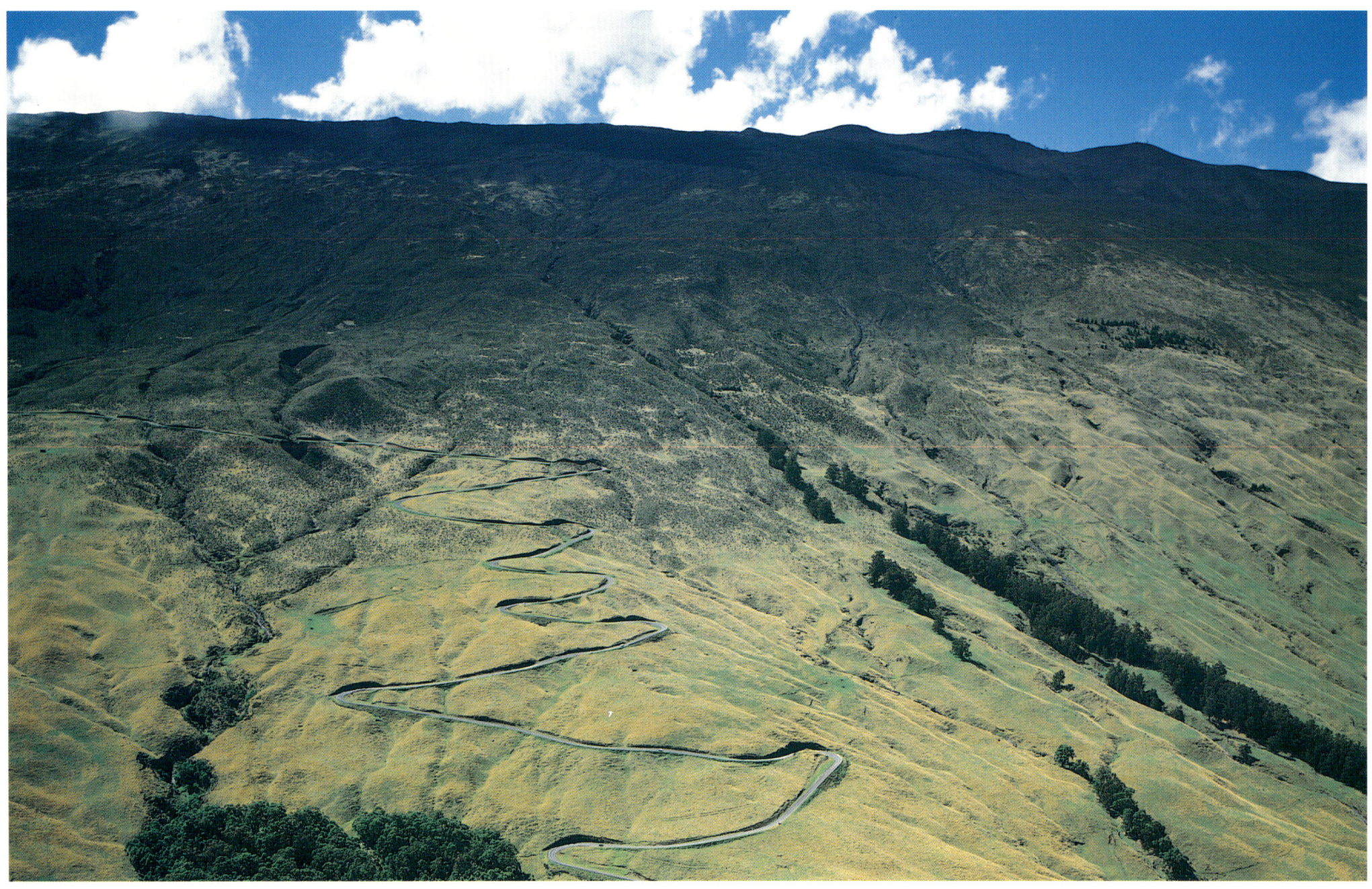

Precipitous turns and breathtaking views greet those traveling the road to Haleakalā, an experience made more adventurous by taking the downhill route by bicycle.

Haleakalā National Park

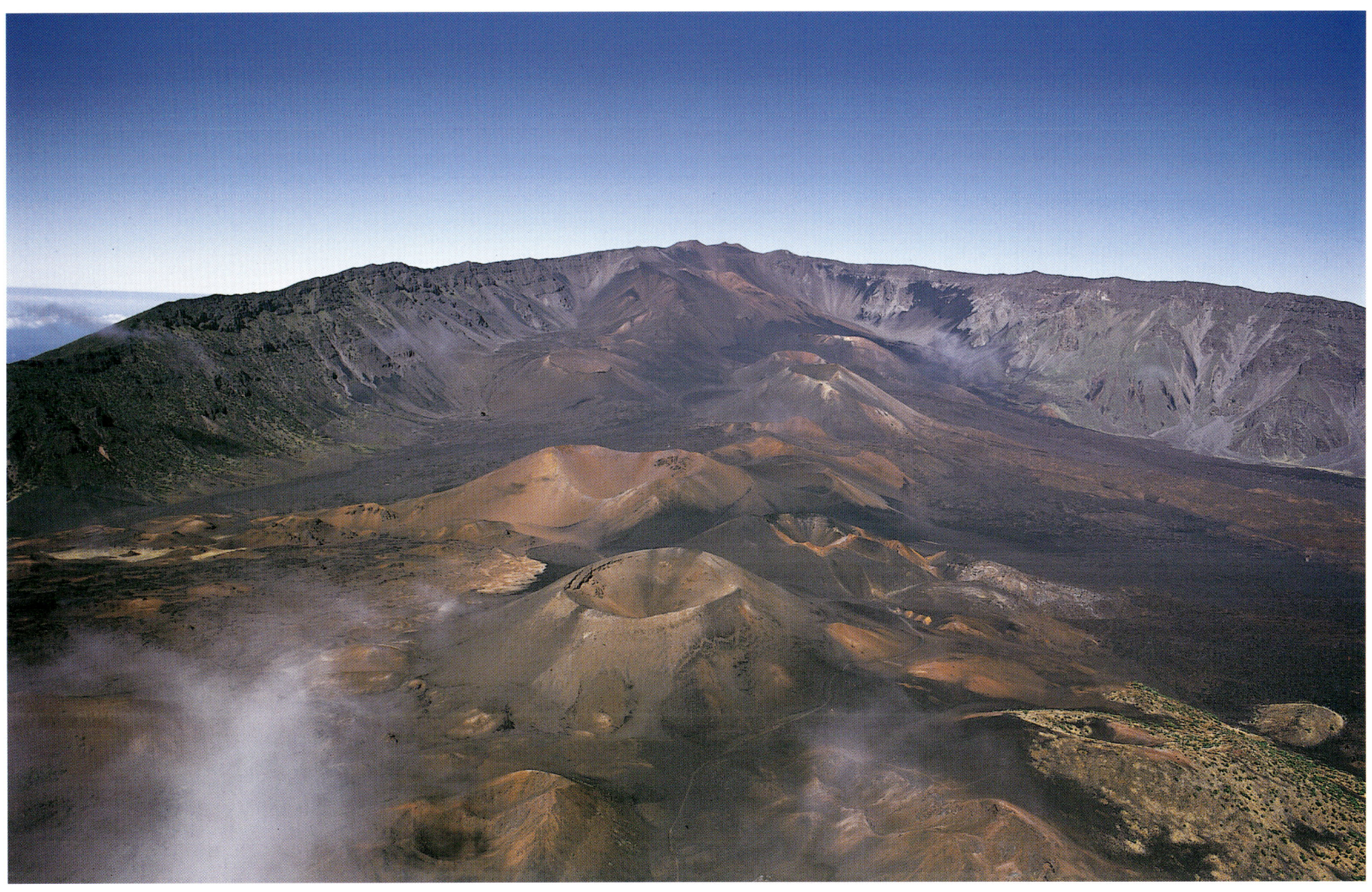

Cinder cones dot the interior of Haleakalā summit, where dry and cold weather nurture unique vegetation and wildlife.

Olinda

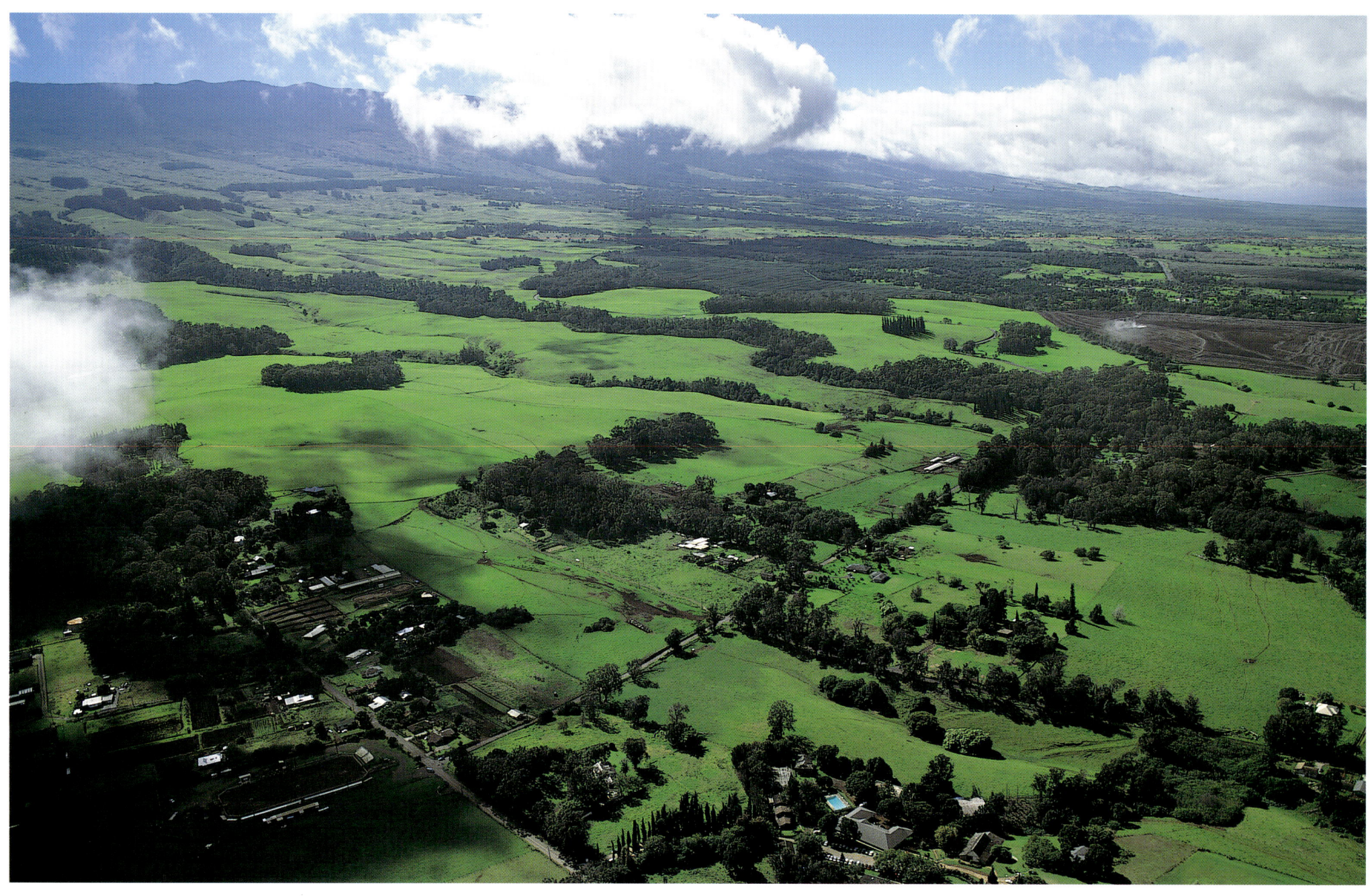

Fragrant eucalyptus-lined roads characterize the Upcountry area of Olinda, site of the yearly rough-and-tumble Makawao Rodeo.

Hāna Coast

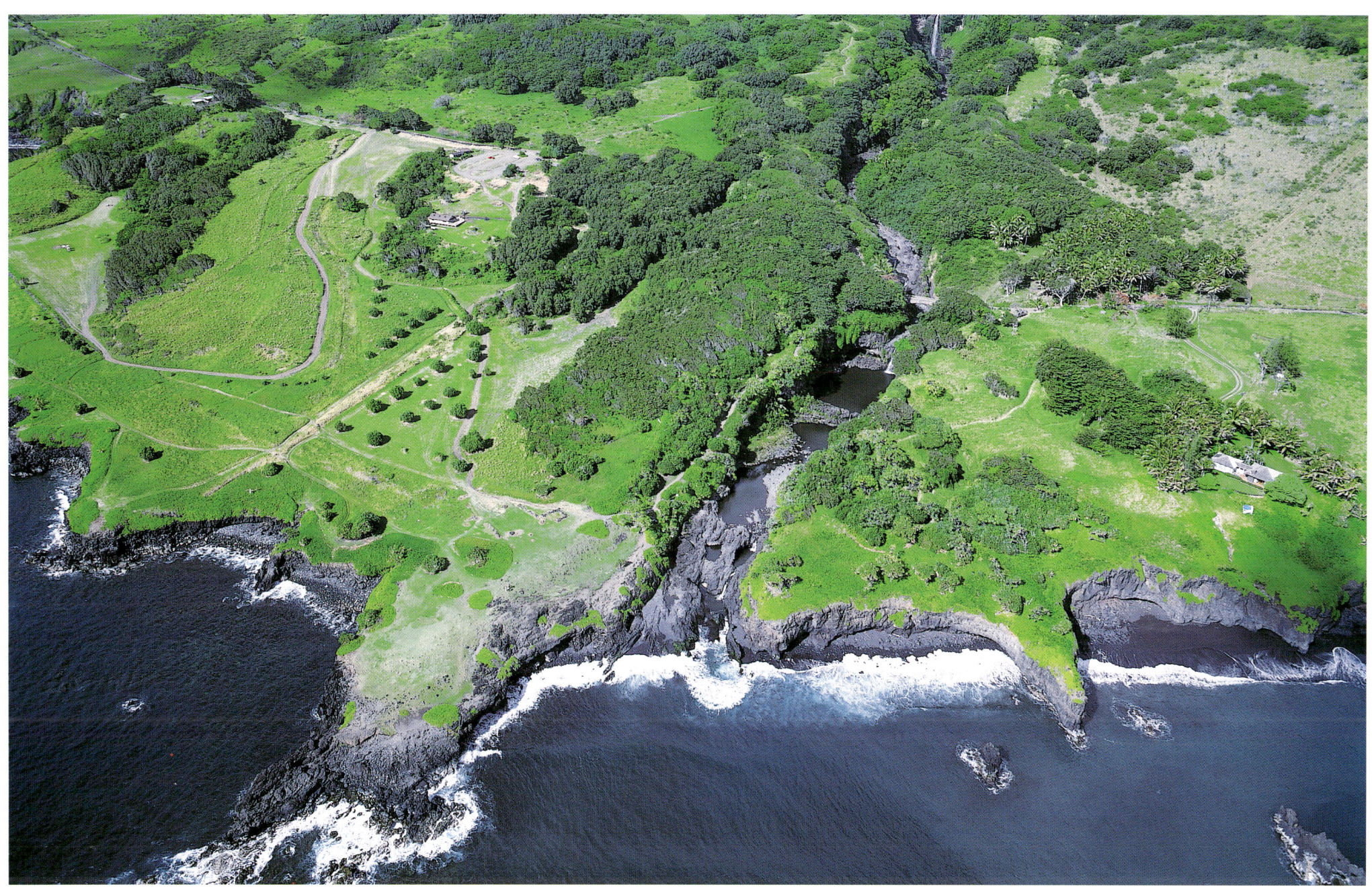

The northeast border of Maui, often called the Hāna coast, is renowned for its imposing cliffs, powerful surf, plentiful waterfalls and flower-strewn rainforest.

Road to Hāna

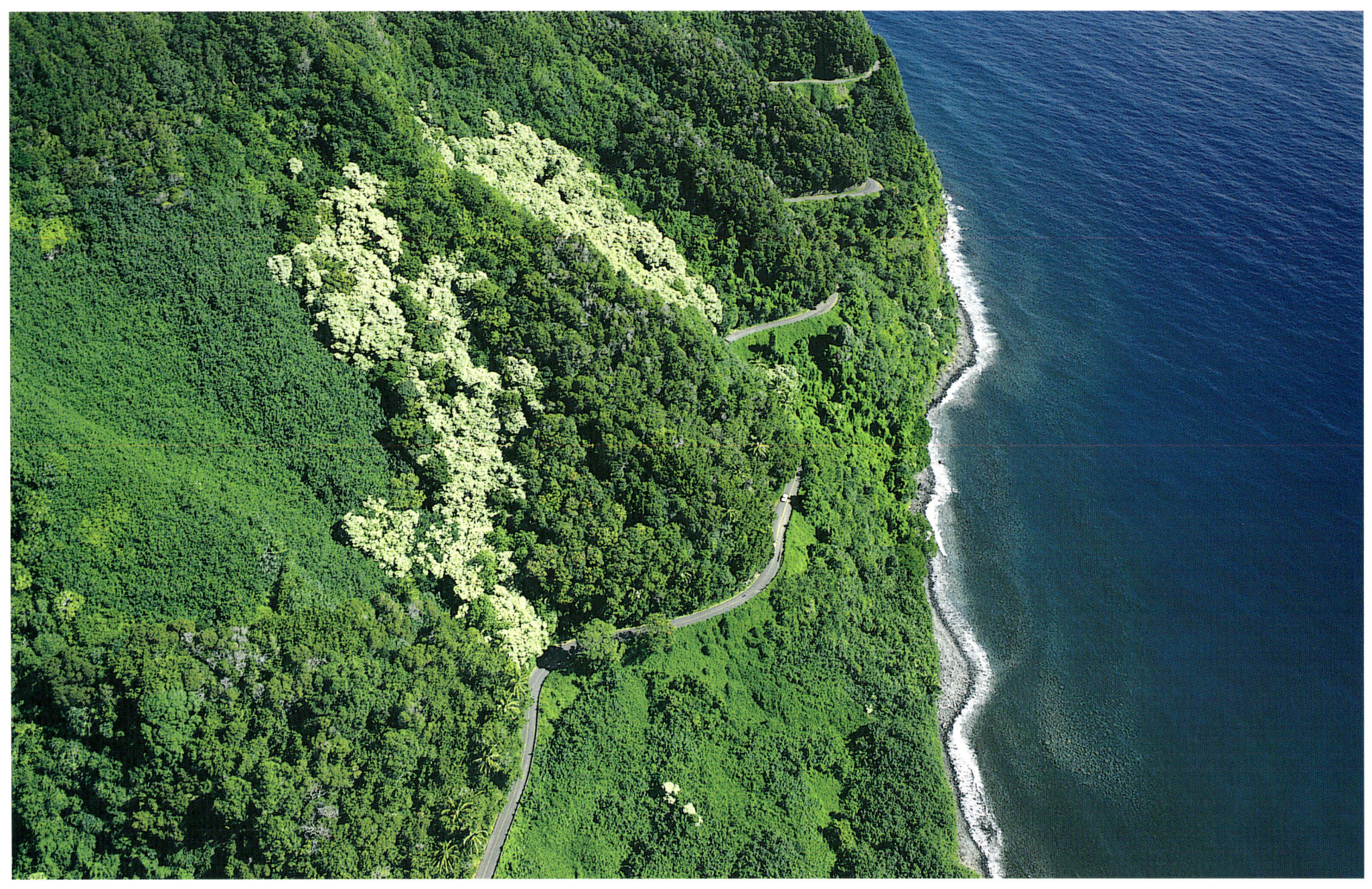

The 52-mile road to Hāna, with its 617 curves and 56 bridges, offers some of the most spectacular vistas in the whole island chain.

Hāna Coast

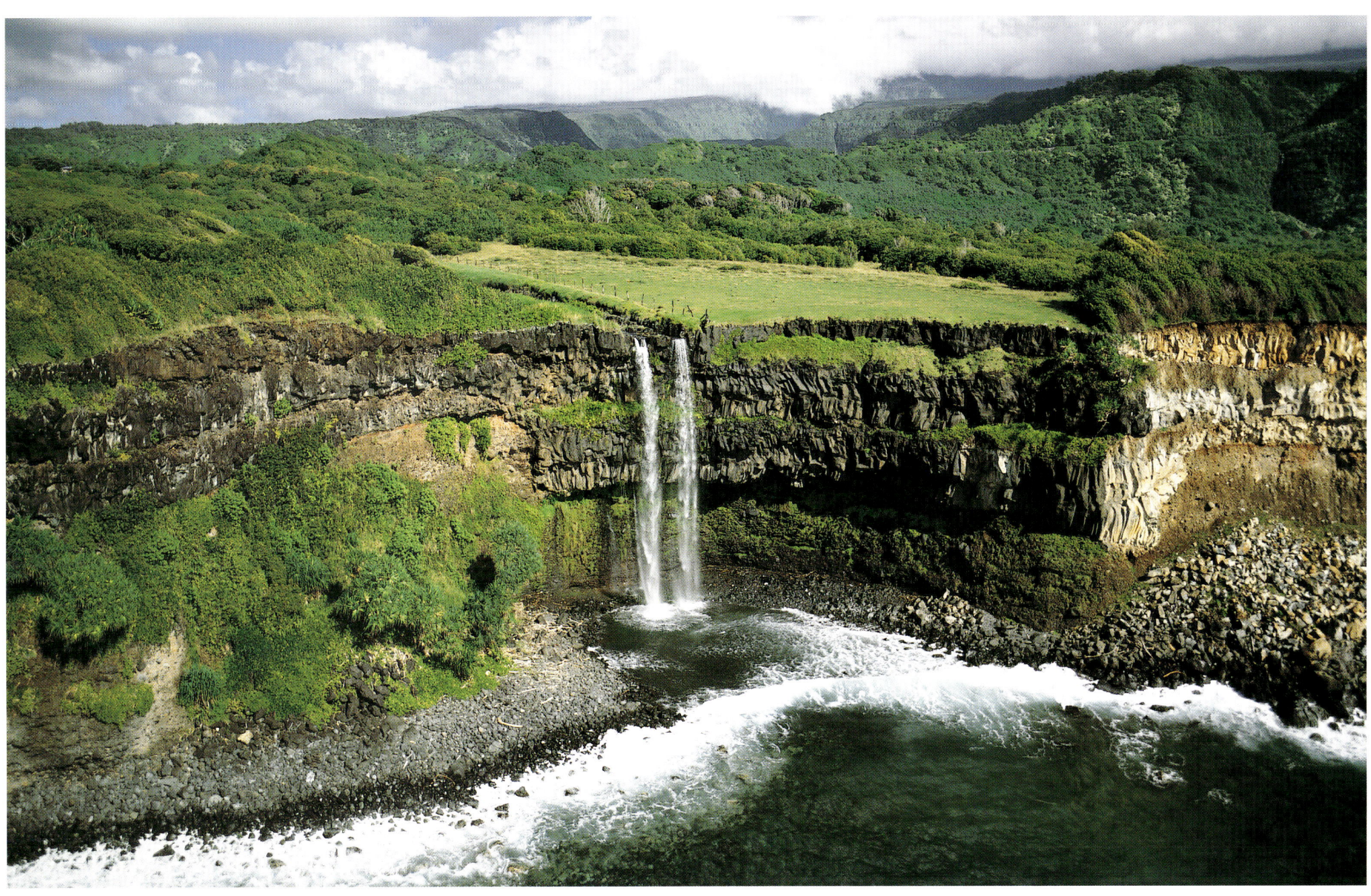

Twin falls tumble into the ocean, forming a shallow pool where salt and fresh water meet.

Waihoʻi Valley

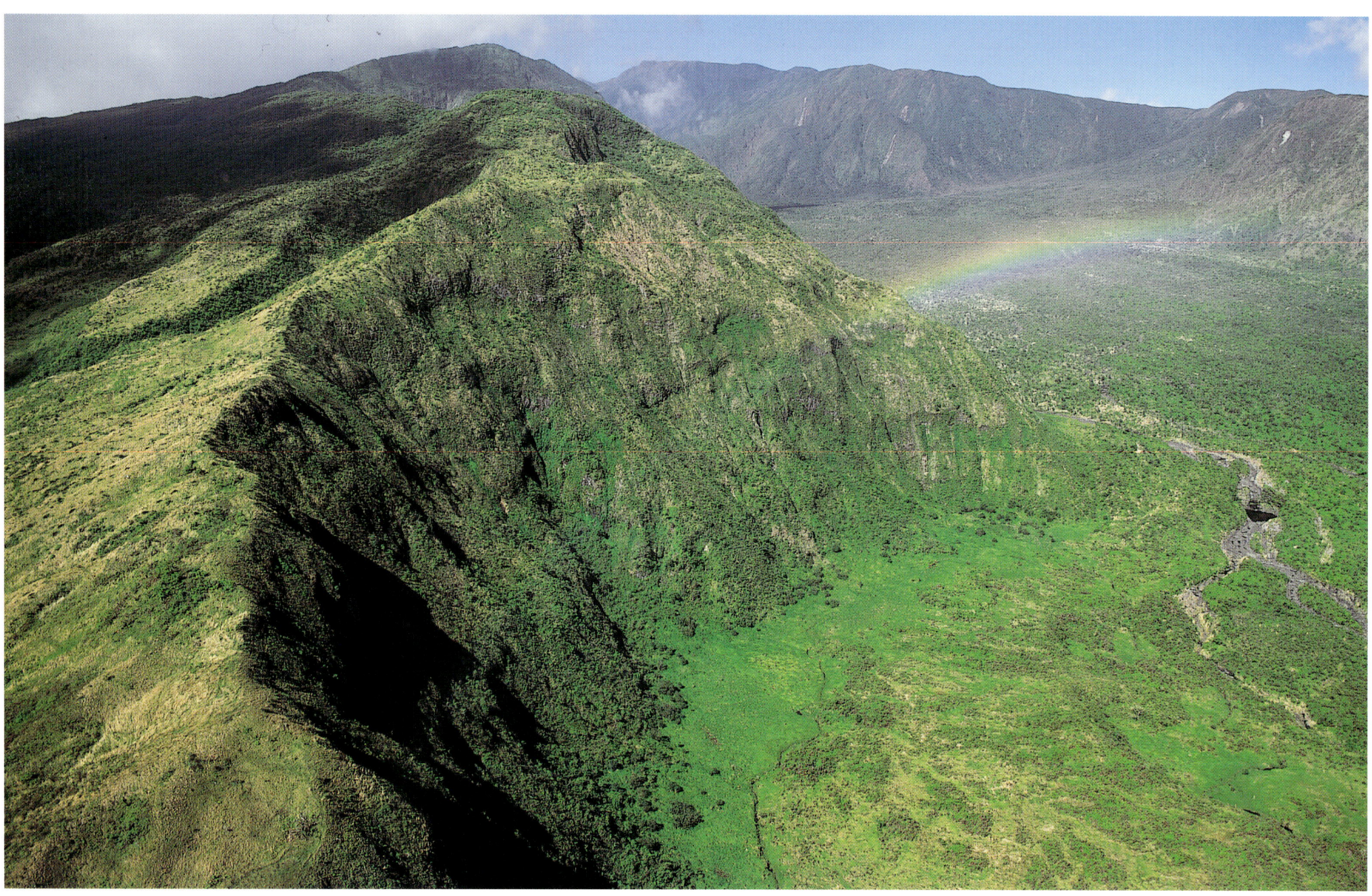

Dramatic Waihoʻi Valley remains an unspoiled habitat for rare Hawaiian birds and plants.

Hāmoa Beach

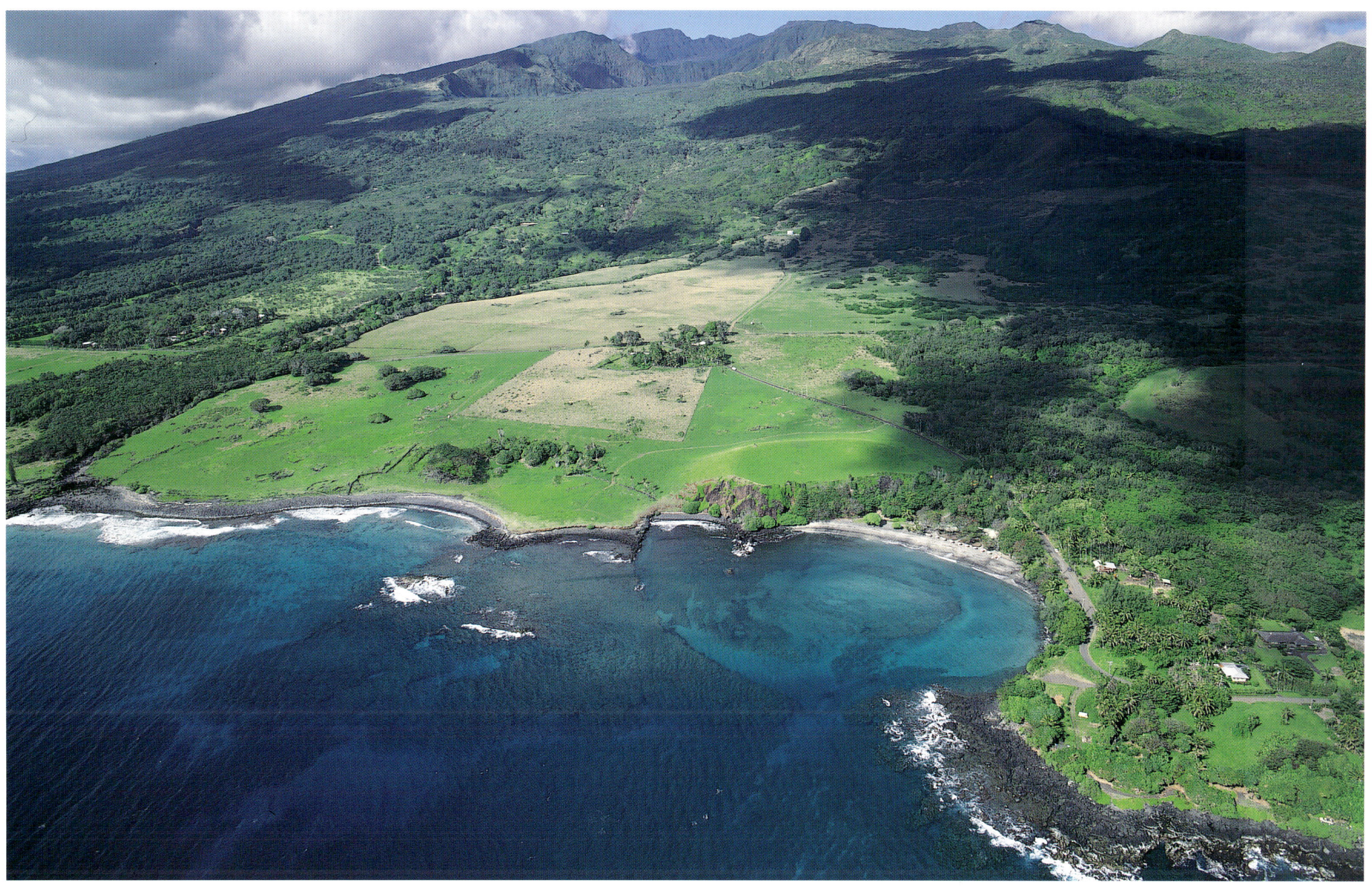

Hāmoa Beach, a restful spot offering surf, sand and serenity, lies tucked within Mōkae Cove.

ʻĀlau Island

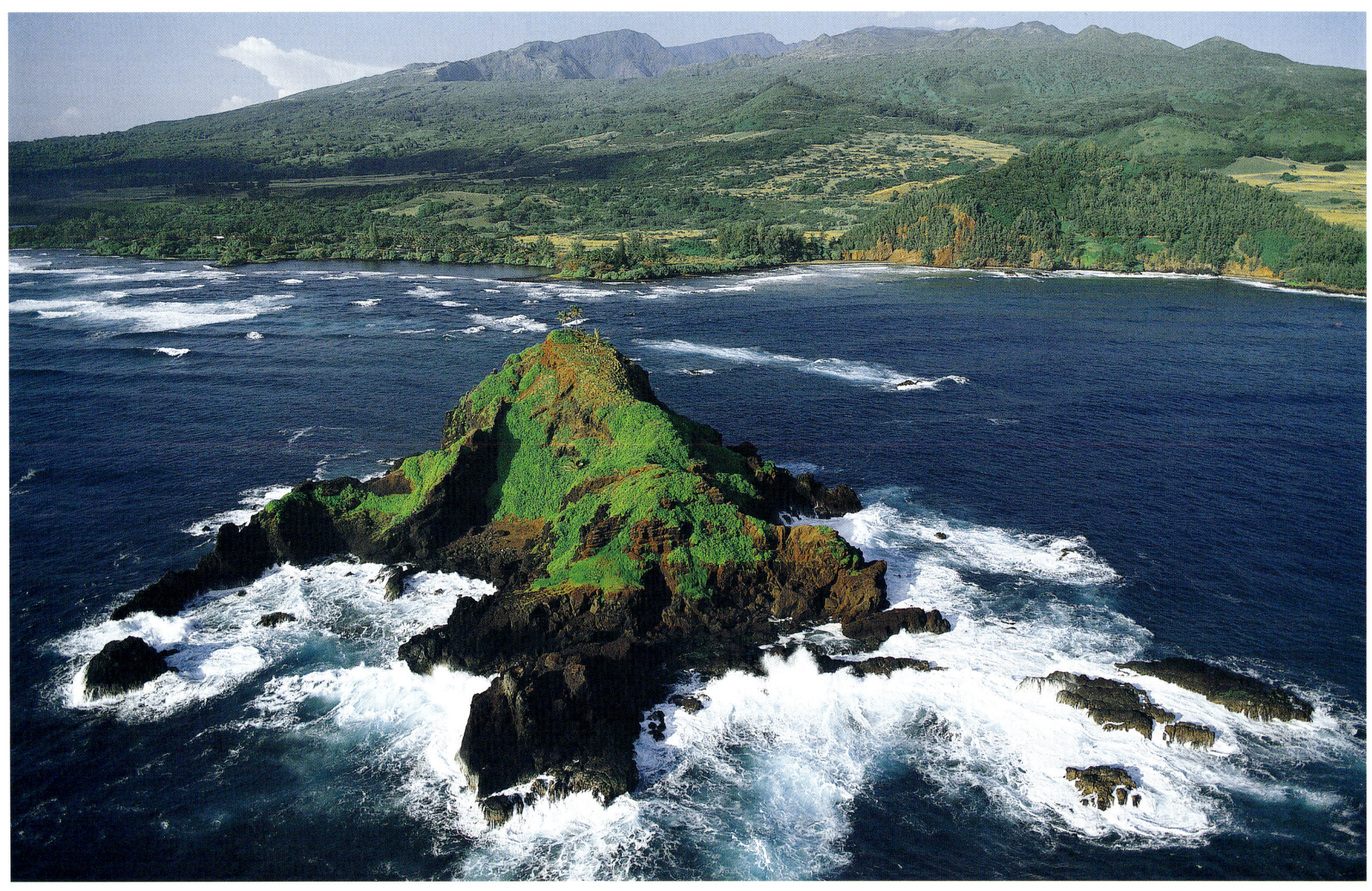

Rough white-water waves pound the seabird sanctuary on ʻĀlau, an island said to have been created by the goddess Pele.

Kaupō

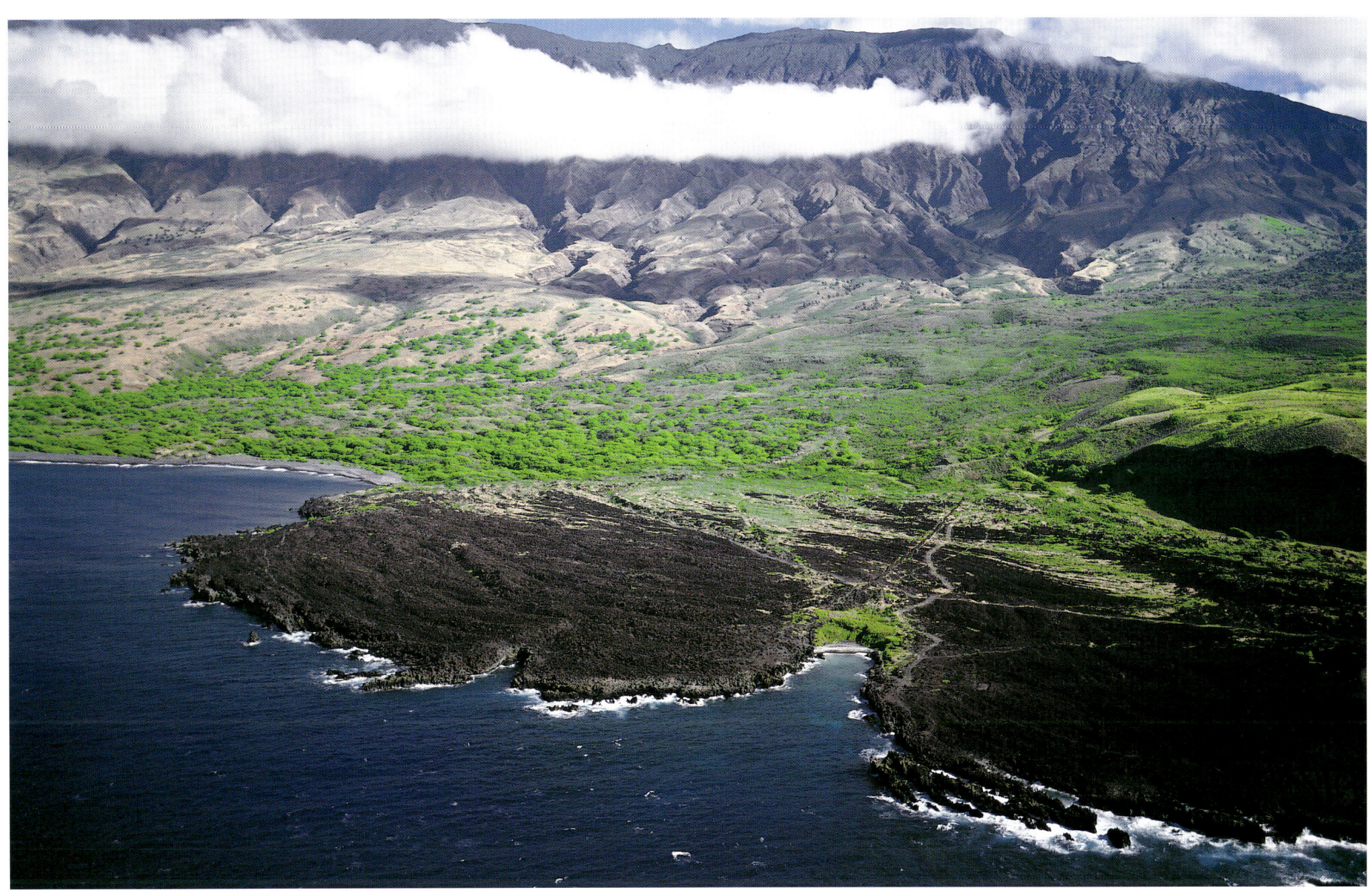

The rugged ranchlands of Kaupō border the verdant end of east Maui.

Manawainui

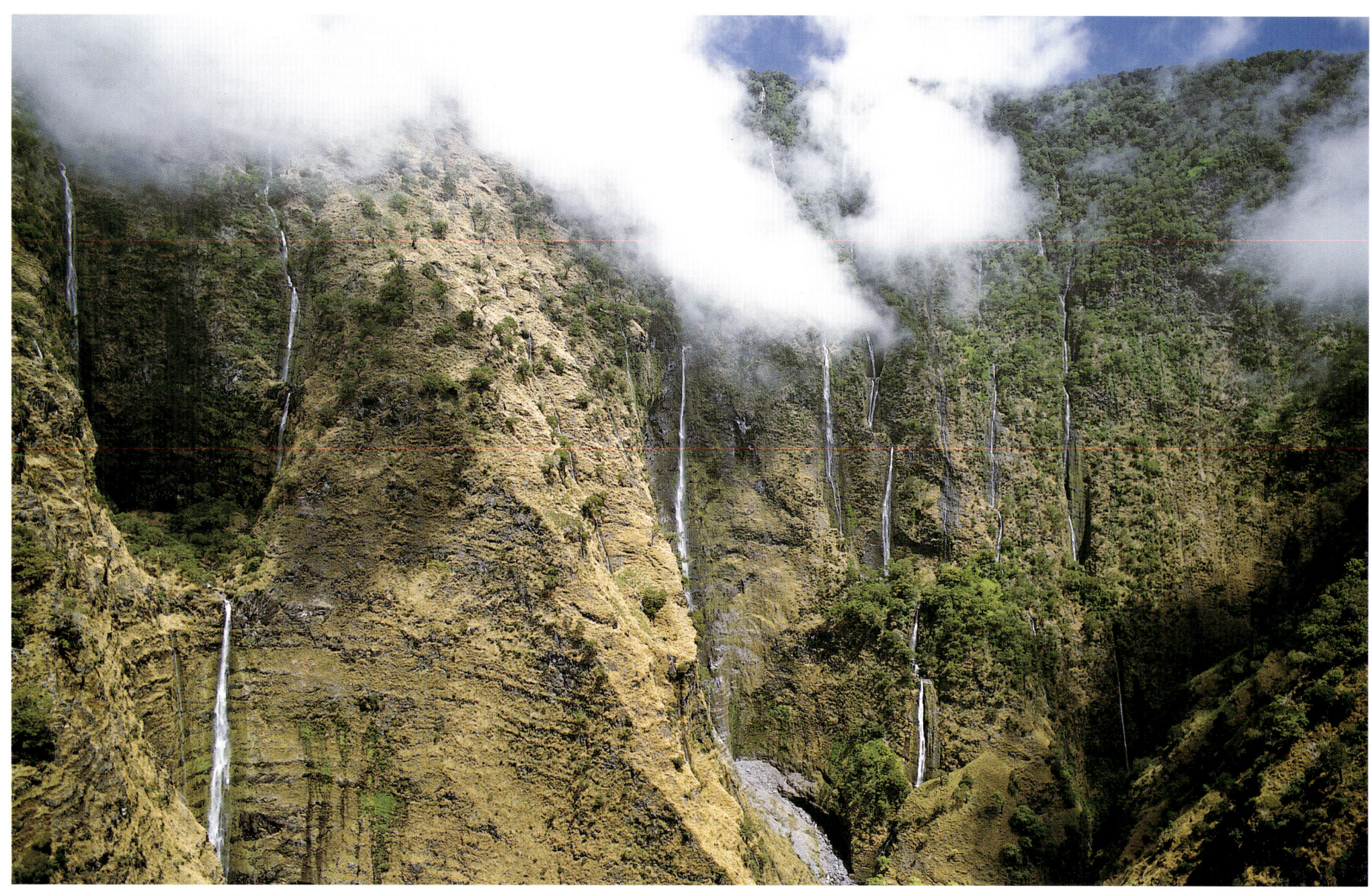

Clouds mask the summit of steep cliffs ribboned with waterfalls at Manawainui Gulch.

ʻUlupalakua

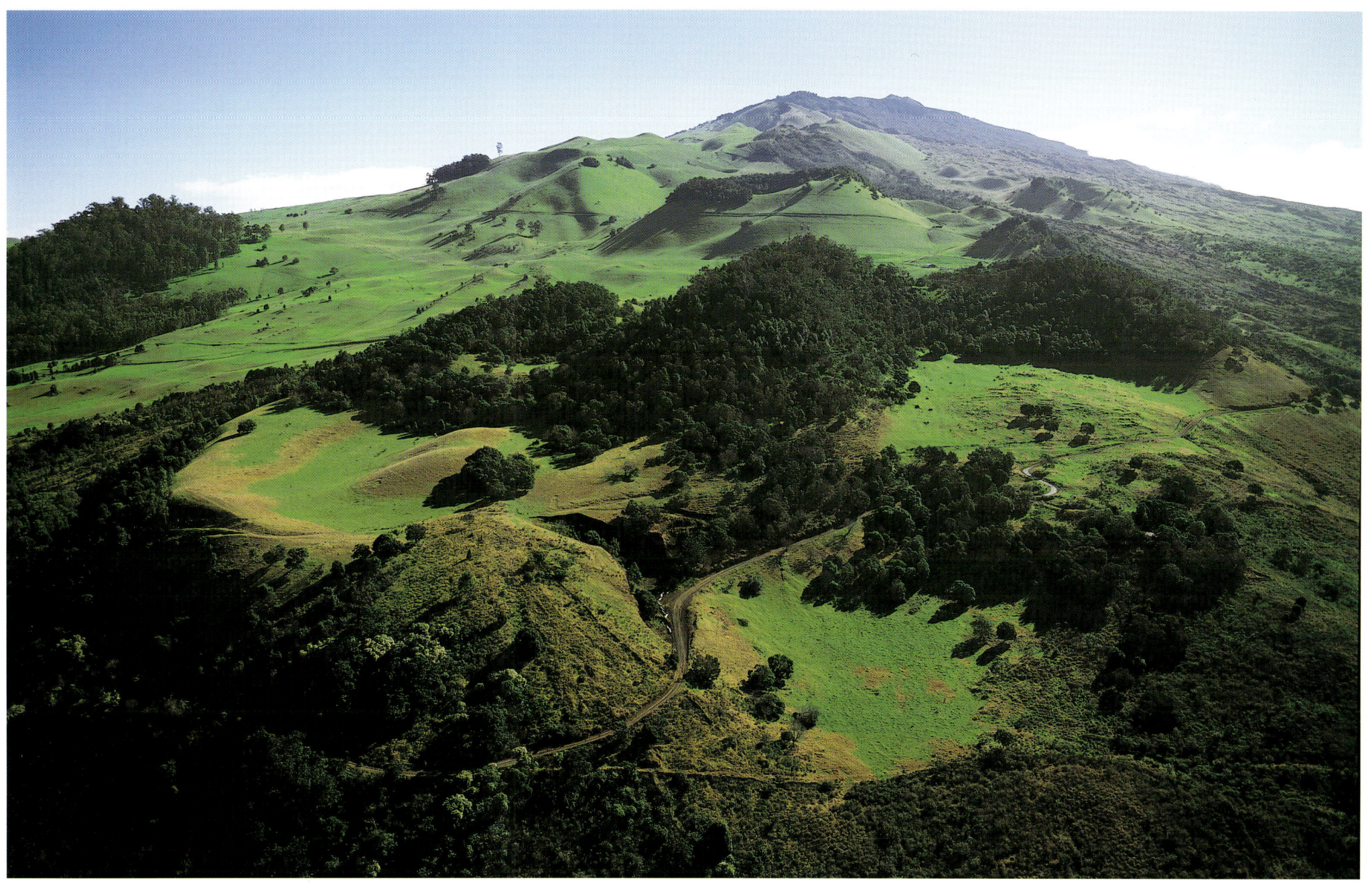

ʻUlupalakua Ranch, not far from Mākena, presents a lush landscape of open spaces and rolling hills.

Molokini Island

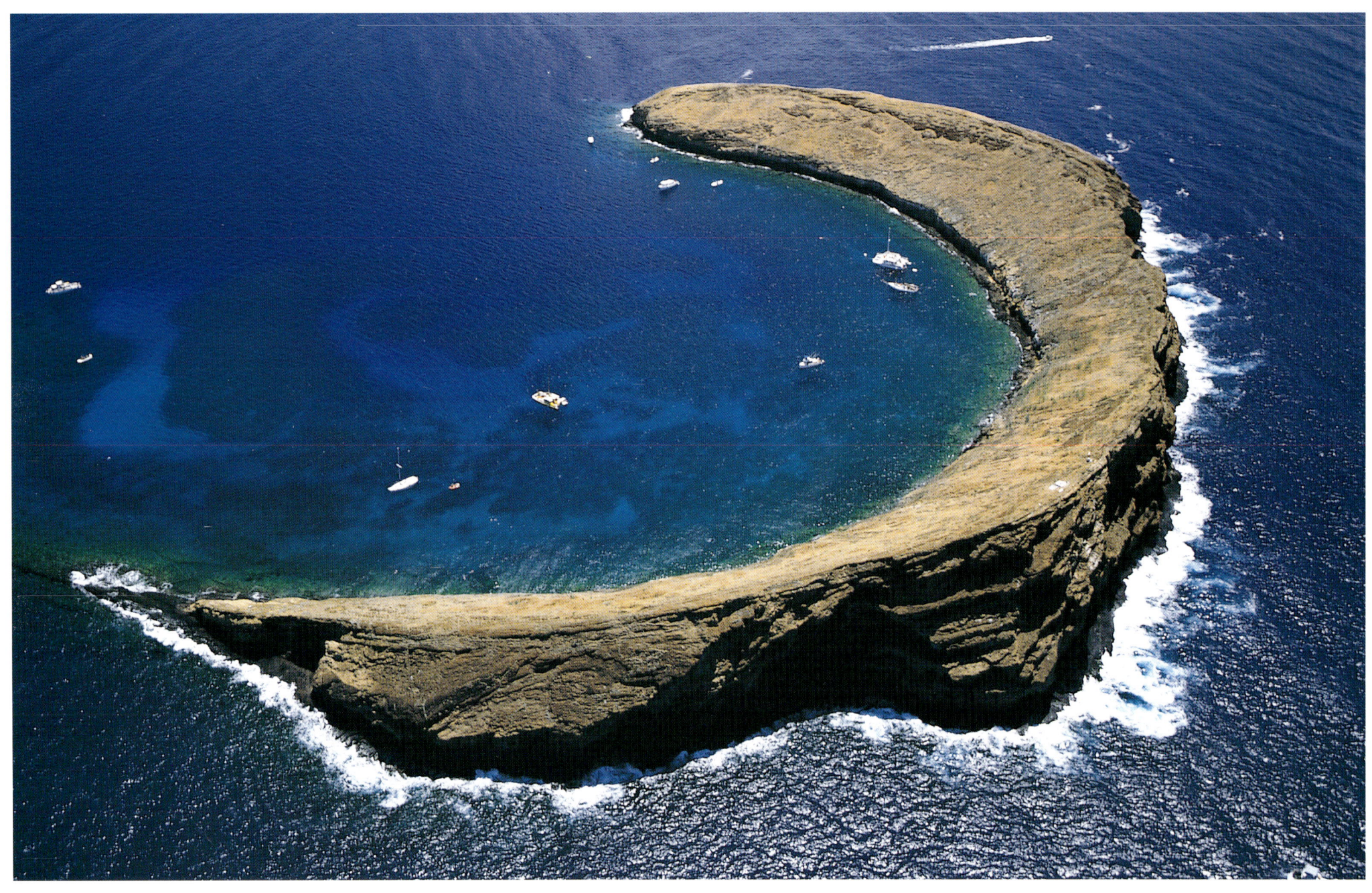

Molokini, three miles off the coast of Maui, acts as a mooring spot for day diving charters. Sand channels can be seen among the coral reefs within the partly-submerged crater.